NOTHING PERSONAL

Seeing Beyond the Illusion of a Separate Self

NOTHING PERSONAL

Seeing Beyond the Illusion of a Separate Self

NIRMALA

Endless Satsang Foundation

This book was created from talks and dialogues held from 1999 to 2004 in Montreal, Tucson, Phoenix, Sedona, Santa Cruz, Palo Alto, Boulder, Seattle, and Dallas. Gratitude is extended to everyone who participated.

The poems in this book are from *Gifts with No Giver: A Love Affair with Truth,* a collection of nondual poetry by Nirmala, which is also available from Endless Satsang Foundation.

Endless Satsang Foundation
endless-satsang.com

Copyright © 2001 by Daniel Erway (Nirmala)

First Edition 2001
Second Edition 2007

ISBN for this edition: 978-0-6151-8767-9

Cover photo: © Andreykuzmin/dreamstime.com

ACKNOWLEDGMENTS

To my wife, Gina, for her limitless love and support. This book would not have happened without her help and the countless hours she spent transcribing, editing, and re-editing these talks until they took on the form of a book. This volume is equally an expression of her wisdom, talent, and gifts.

To my teacher and friend, Adyashanti, for his guidance and perspective, which have opened ever-new vistas in this vastness of being.

And to my teacher and friend, Neelam, who first opened my heart to the spacious love we all share.

Finally, with gratitude for the blessings of truth brought to this world by Ramana Maharshi and H.W. L. Poonja (Papaji).

CONTENTS

PART 3
Being

PART 4
The Mystery of Awareness

PART 5
The End of Suffering

PART 6
Approaching the Mystery

PART 7
Two Simple Instructions

PART 8
Awakening

PART 9
Living Life as a Question

FOREWORD

After years of Zen practice my teacher asked me to begin teaching, and she gave me these words of advice: Always tell the truth and speak from your own experience. In the years since, I have found this advice to be crucial to both teachers and students alike. By inquiring into truth, we are led ever deeper into the unknown—beyond beliefs and ideas to the very core of who and what we are. This inquiry takes the highest degree of integrity and fearlessness we can muster; it challenges us by taking us out of our heads and into the heart of our deepest experience of being, which is beyond limitations of body, mind, and conditioning. Telling the truth is the secret of all true spirituality, and in order to tell the truth, you must find out what truth is. It is my experience of Nirmala that he embodies my teacher's advice both as an individual and as a teacher.

In the West, we are in need of a practical mysticism that reveals not only the deepest core of being but also addresses how to act and relate from that core in this event called "life." In order to accomplish this, we do not need another set of how-to instructions, which are so popular within our modern consumer culture of quick fixes. What we need is an ever-deepening inquiry into how spirit dances as this very life, for what we call "life" is but an expression of spirit and therefore fully spirit itself. As I often say to my own students, "First you awaken out of life, then you awaken as life itself."

The beauty of this collection of Nirmala's talks and dialogues is that it covers much of the spectrum of spiritual awakening, from the initial experience of one's true nature to the practical challenges, which always call for a deeper seeing and deeper understanding of how spirit manifests as all of life and beyond. Within these talks and dialogues you, the reader, will find Nirmala to be a living invitation to look within.

What is appealing about Nirmala is his humility and lack of pretense, which welcomes whatever arises within the field of experience. In the midst of this welcoming is always an invitation to inquire deeply within, to the core of who and what you are. Again and again, Nirmala points the questions back to the questioner and beyond to the very source of existence itself—to the faceless awareness that holds both the question and the questioner in a timeless embrace.

I invite you into these talks and dialogues—not as a spectator but as an intimate participant. Look within and see exactly who and what is doing the looking. In a timeless instant, now, become aware of yourself as awareness itself.

Adyashanti
March, 2001

INTRODUCTION

Unlike most books, this one is not meant to add to your knowledge or understanding. It is about the Truth that cannot be spoken or written. Although the Truth cannot be contained in this or any other book, each word written here is intended to point you toward that Truth. Many of the words and ideas may seem paradoxical or contradictory because what they point to is larger than our conceptual frameworks. Many questions are asked, which are not answered anywhere in the book. Find out what the experience is like to ask yourself these questions, even if they leave you emptier of knowledge and understanding. In this emptying, you just may discover what you are looking for.

The Truth is revealed when we allow ourselves to not know, so I invite you to set aside all that you know for the time being and allow yourself to look with innocent eyes at what the words are attempting to unveil. Take the time to experience the unspoken truth in each section before moving on to the next. Resist the temptation to read these words with your mind, which is likely to rush right past the Truth. Allow the words to sink into your heart and reveal the truth of who you are.

PART 1

Moving from the Mind into the Heart

mind finds a path
to struggle along
never reaching the goal
heart knows it already rests
in the path of something wonderful
it cannot escape
>*mind seeks to hold on to*
>*a still point*
>*of final understanding*
>*heart knows it is being held*
>*by an unmoving whirlwind*
>*that it will never comprehend*

mind tries to feel safe enough
to allow love
out into the open
heart knows love is never cautious
and cannot be kept secret
once all hope of refuge is abandoned

Finding What Doesn't Come and Go

We all want the same thing: we all want to be happy. We look everywhere for happiness—in experiences, in possessions, in other people, in pleasures, in success, but we come up empty-handed because they are not the *source* of happiness. We have to go to the source. But how? How do we find the source? All of these things we are chasing after come and go, so we must look to that which doesn't come and go—that is the source. It turns out that the source of everything is also who you are. You are the source of everything, but don't take my word for it. Let's discover this together. Since the source of everything doesn't come and go, it must be here right now, in this very moment. So, let's look into this moment and see what is present in it and what, among the many things that are present, does not come and go.

Let's start simply by noticing the sensations that are present. Just for a moment, be present to the ongoing flow of sensation. One of the things you'll notice is that sensations are always changing. Your sensory experience is never the same from one moment to the next. Nevertheless, there is a continuity to them; they flow from one to the other. So, while sensations do not qualify as something that doesn't come and go, they are woven together in a way that gives an impression of continuity.

In contrast, notice the lack of continuity in the experience of thought. Thoughts are very fluid. When you are present to your thoughts, you discover how unsubstantial, incomplete, and disjointed they are relative to the experience of sensations. Memories, which are just thoughts about the past, are a good example of this. You never have a truly complete memory of an experience because it would take as long as the experience itself. Most of our memories are like still photos or a series of photos highlighting something that was important or stood out about an experience. They are whittled-down, highly-edited versions of what happened. Like an amateur movie, they are jumbled and patched together, often without even a thread to the story line.

Notice for a moment how these highly-edited thoughts differ from sensations. Like sensations, thought is always changing, but the changes can happen much more quickly. In thought, you can move the furniture around instantly. Thoughts allow us to play outside the boundaries of space and time; however, thought is not as well constructed as sensory data or the material world.

Another difference between thought and sensory data is that thought is always either a memory about the past or a fantasy about the future, while sensory impressions happen in the present. Thoughts appear in the present, but their content is always about the past or future because there is never enough time in the present to have a thought about the present. You can't think that fast. By the time you think about an event, it is already in the past.

The difference between thought and sensory data is obvious to us, but it's not to everyone. Some people in mental hospitals can't tell the difference. Many of their thoughts are real to them. They can't distinguish between a thought and a thing. The ability to distinguish this makes it possible for us to function in the world. Some thoughts are so convincing that we scare ourselves, but we can usually tell the difference between thought and sensory data. The reason thoughts can be very convincing is that they are often based on previous sensory experience.

It's good to notice that thoughts and memories don't have as much solidity or consistency as we'd like to think. They are always changing. I challenge you to have the same thought for even fifteen seconds. Even your memory of a particular event is always changing. For example, the memory of your first date with your spouse will not be the same after twenty years of marriage as it was a week after you met, and certainly not the same if you divorce. Many studies have shown how surprisingly inaccurate memory is. When ten people witness an event, you get ten versions of it, none of which match the actual event. Thoughts or memories definitely don't qualify either as that which doesn't come and go and therefore cannot be the source of happiness, peace, and love.

Now, just for fun, I invite you to have a particular thought—
the thought of "I" or "me." Really experience this "I." Does it
have the quality of something real, or is it more like a memory,
something that is incomplete? What does your character look like
in your internal movies and how accurate is that? Has it ever been
several days since you looked in the mirror, and when you did, it
surprised you because it didn't match your idea of what you look
like? You'll notice that you can never get a consistent image of this
"I"; you can't pin it down. You can't find it, any more than you
can find the thought you had five minutes ago.

Another thing you'll notice is how the "I" fluctuates.
Sometimes you have a positive self-image and sometimes not. We
have all had moments of being caught in the idea of being a
hopeless nobody. You're really believing that, and then an
attractive person shows interest in you, and you forget all about
that story of being a nobody. Or, have you ever been walking
along with an upbeat "I" thought, when someone criticizes you
and suddenly you're stuck with a dejected "I" thought? This "I"
thought has the same fluidity and amorphous quality of every
thought and memory.

Although the "I" is often associated with the body, it can't be
the body because we say things like "I have bad eyesight" rather
than "I am bad eyesight." Whenever we refer to the body, there is
still something called "I" present as well. Clearly, the body is a part
of physical reality; it's a thing that can be referred to. However, the
"I" doesn't refer to any *thing*. You can have an elaborate story
about "I," and you can refer to that story and worry about how
that story is going, but there is no thing that all of that refers to.
"I" is just a lot of memories patched together to make what we call
a self-image, which is an accurate description of it—it's an image.
It turns out that the "I" is just thoughts about "I."

Really notice this moment's experience of "I." No matter how
hard you try, it is nothing more than a movie clip. What is even
stranger is that you are usually included in the movie clip, when
you rarely actually see yourself, except in a mirror. Most of us have

never seen ourselves eating breakfast, for instance, but we all have images of what we look like doing that. We completely manufacture images of ourselves doing things. We manufacture memories and call them "me." Then, we work at improving our self-image, when all that can accomplish is to improve this memory! In our culture, we focus on creating a positive self-image, as if an image has any power. No one's self-image has ever accomplished anything.

We also have a fantasy that our self-image is what people see, when what they see is *their* image of us. No one relates to your image of you—they can't see your internal image. Somehow, we think that our self-image will protect us or make us well liked. The truth of this moment is that your self-image isn't doing anything. Your self-image isn't what is hearing these words or having the thoughts you are having. Your self-image is itself a thought. No matter how polished your self-image is, you can't send it to work while you stay home. Hearing and thinking are present, but the mystery is: who or what is doing these things? If you are honest, you can't assign credit for that to what you call "I" or "me."

Have you also noticed that there are big gaps in this thought called "me," when you forget to be somebody? You get engrossed in something and forget to maintain your self-image. Even when people are holding a self-image of being depressed, there are moments when they forget to feel depressed because their attention is elsewhere. If we're looking for that which doesn't come and go, this "I" certainly doesn't qualify. It qualifies even less as the source of happiness than anything in sensory experience, so all the time spent trying to improve it doesn't pay off. It's not the object of our search.

So, what else is present right here, right now—besides sensations, experiences, thoughts, feelings, and "you"—that doesn't come and go? What is it that notices the sensory data? What is it that hears the internal dialogues? What is it that notices the self-images and isn't fooled by them? What is the source of all the thoughts, even the "I" thought? It's not something you can sense. You can't find it in the body or in the brain, and yet it is here, right now. And— here's where it gets even spookier—you can't even think about it. Your thoughts about who you are will never adequately represent who you are.

There is this Mystery that thinks and sees and feels and has a body. This Mystery has the fundamental quality of awareness: it is aware of thought, feeling, and sensation. So, even if you haven't been paying attention to anything I've just said, I guarantee that paying attention has still been happening. There was something mysterious that was aware of the sensations and thoughts that I asked you to be aware of. There was something checking your present experience or your memories to see if what I was saying was true for you. Even if that wasn't happening, there was something that was paying attention to something else. It turns out that it is not "you" who is noticing these sensations or noticing this poorly produced movie called "me." It's not "you" that is watching the movie called "me," and yet watching is happening.

This mysterious something is like a flashlight. I call it that because there is a quality of brightness to it. Whatever you bring your attention to becomes lit up by this Awareness. If you become aware of your hands, a brightness comes to your hands. But this brightness is not yours; it's not "you." There is something that is either hearing my words or ignoring my words. What is present even when you are distracted by some irrelevant thought? What is noticing the distracting thoughts? What is this mysterious brightness that is experiencing the endless variations of thought and sensation? What is present in all of these experiences?

If you assign a "me" to it, you create a middleman. This "me" is never the experiencer; it can only be an added layer of experience in the form of a thought about "me." The experiencer doesn't go away; it just experiences this moment with an extra layer called "me." In some ways this truth is very humbling. It's a big demotion for the "me" to discover that it is just an additional, poorly formed layer of thought, which can never be made to be consistent or reliable. No idea you have ever had about yourself has ever lasted.

No matter how elaborate your fantasy of being someone is, you have never succeeded in completely hiding that which does not come and go *and* you have never done any harm to it. "You" can't mess this life up because "you" aren't living it. We think that if there isn't this "me" taking care of life, it's going to fall apart, but it never has been "you" that has been taking care of your life. So, what will you trust? Will you trust this fantasy that has never accomplished anything or this Mystery that has actually been living every moment of life?

But thought is powerful.

Thought is powerful in the realm of thought. Thought can do serious damage to your self-image. So what? Just take your self-image right now and dress it in tattered clothes. Now you have a self-image of a homeless person. The thought, itself, is not the problem but how caught you are in it. If you are caught in it, it doesn't matter if it is a thought of heaven or hell. People suffer just as much over their thoughts about how wonderful things might be as they do over their thoughts about what might go wrong.

If you mistake your thoughts for something that doesn't come and go, they can be very convincing. The story called "me" is like a record you play over and over again. We think, "that must be me because that's what I think of when I think of me." We get lulled by the habitual nature of thought. But if you are honest, you'll see that there are moments when you forget the story—you forget that particular train of thought called "me"—and Awareness is still here, even when "you" are not.

* * *

I feel tense because I feel like I always need to plan.

The simplest way to address this is for you to check: can you find this someone who has to have a plan? Can you find her right now?

No.

So, if she isn't here and has never been here, then there is this mystery: who has done all that planning? Where did all that come from?

It came from fear.

But who experienced this fear? If this "you" doesn't really exist, then what we are calling fear is not something you did either. That also is something that just happened. This is really good news: you are not to blame even for the "you" that is afraid. This is a big relief. You're off the hook.

Beyond that, there is also the possibility of getting curious: who or what is hearing these words right now? It's obviously not "you" but something much bigger. *That* has always been the one deciding when to plan and when not to, and it will decide if you will plan tomorrow or not. Just get curious about *that*.

* * *

What about free will and choice?

Once you recognize that there is no "me," then there can't be something called "my" will. But there is will—it's just not "yours."

You mean, I'm not making any choices?

What you think you are has never made a choice, and yet choices are being made all the time.

Who's making them?

This is a good question! This is a huge mystery, which has been going on every day of your life. Choices have happened without your having anything to do with it. This raises the question, who or what is living your life?

The Truth About Thought

Let's take a look at thought. Do you have a choice about what thoughts come? Do you decide to have a thought and then it shows up, or does it just show up? If you have never decided to have even a single thought, can you still call them "your" thoughts? How can they be your responsibility if they aren't yours? They just showed up. Just notice the nature of thoughts and where they come from. Then look even closer: how many of your thoughts are even true? How reliable are they?

Once you realize that most of your thoughts are lies and not worthy guides, you lose interest in them. Some thoughts and words are useful, such as "please pass the butter," but most do not refer to anything real or serve any purpose. Once you see this, you can't be bothered with them anymore. They can't compete with the richness of the present moment. The difference between thoughts and the present moment is like the difference between fantasy and reality. As nice as a fantasy might be, it never has the aliveness, vividness, or dimensionality of reality. Thoughts actually cloud reality, forming a layer of illusion between ourselves and the present moment. Thoughts—even pleasant fantasies and dreams—are like a veil, hiding the true beauty of this moment.

Thought is just a sliver of the now, so if you are too focused on that, you miss everything else that is arising in the now.

* * *

You say it is important to be present to everything. So, should you be present even to this illusion called thought?

Yes. Then, it becomes possible to consider who is having these thoughts. It is just being honest to admit that they aren't "your" thoughts. When you actually look in this moment, you can't find such a thing as "you."

When you are fully present to your thoughts, they don't change, but you are more able to be present to everything else—to the rest of the Mystery. When thoughts are finally recognized as just one aspect of experience, they naturally get relegated to a minor, supporting role. Thought can be a handy tool, but it has never been the whole story. Of course, the mind will put up a fuss over this demotion. Find out what happens if you just stay present even to this. Then it is possible to realize that thought, itself, is an incredible mystery.

Mind Games

The source of suffering is the discrepancy between our thoughts (including the thought "me") and the truth of here and now. You would think that we wouldn't be that interested in something that causes so much suffering, and yet we spend a great deal of time sprucing up our thoughts and fantasies.

Just as we are entranced by television, we are entranced by the mind. Have you ever noticed how similar television is to the mind? Just like in the mind, on television, something new is always appearing to grab our attention. Because the mind's job is to scan the environment and notice anything new and different, it is no wonder the mind finds the constant change on the television screen engrossing.

In the real world, on the other hand, life unfolds slowly and organically. If you took a video camera with you on a 30-minute walk and left it on, you'd have a really bad movie. Can you imagine renting that at Blockbuster video?—"Life at Normal Speed." Just notice how attracted the mind is to special effects, drama, and speeded-up versions of life. Even though our thoughts and fantasies are the basis of our suffering, we become engaged with them because, like television and movies, they are entertaining.

Eventually, as with any other addiction, we come to see that our thoughts and fantasies are not very satisfying or fulfilling. Like watching television for hours on end, they leave us feeling empty. Fortunately, there is a handy alternative to the emptiness of thought: here and now. All that is required is to show up in your life. If you go for a walk, show up for the walk; if it is time to brush your teeth, show up for that. To show up in your life, you just have to pay attention to it. Just notice *what is* right now, without referring to some memory of it. Showing up is very simple—no preparation is needed and you can't get it wrong.

Spiritual practices are the opposite of MTV. They help you tune down the noise and distractions. The mind is like a galloping horse, always off after the next enticing fantasy or memory. It is endlessly grasping after something that isn't real. Spiritual practices rein in that galloping horse, and that helps you show up in your life. What's so surprising is how satisfying that is. It's like the difference between eating a dozen cookies and eating a nourishing meal. As one of my teachers, Richard Clarke, once said, "You can never get enough of what does not satisfy."

Nothing the mind presents is satisfying or nourishing. There is nothing in the mind to compare to this moment as long as you take in all of the moment and not just some highly-edited version of it. That is where you will find real nourishment and aliveness. The joy of what is here right now far surpasses any memory or fantasy.

* * *

Is the mind always confused, and why do we listen to it?

Let me ask you, is your mind always confused?

More and more.

When you start yearning for the Truth—yearning to know who you really are—then the mind spends a lot of time in confusion. Why do *you* keep going back to it?

Habit.

Yes. That is really the truth. Is the Heart present right now?

It must be.

The mind can figure that much out. Tell me, what do you want?

Freedom, but I'm afraid of the giving up, the letting go, the change.

How badly do you want it? Is it worth feeling confused much of the time? What if that was just the nature of the mind's experience of Truth. What if the confusion never gets resolved in the sense that there is finally a knowing? What if the not-knowing just gets bigger and bigger?

That's scary.

To the mind, that is very scary because it has less of a role. It means letting go of dreams and hopes and desires too. Is it worth it? Do you want Freedom that bad?

My heart does.

That's the truth. The one thing I can do is reassure you that it is very normal to feel confused and afraid.

That makes sense. There's so much to let go of. I guess there is a part of me that doesn't want to.

So, let's make it simpler: everything that you are talking about letting go of—have you ever really *had* any of it?

I've never had any of it!

Did you have to let go of believing in Santa Claus?

No.

But there was a certain point when the truth about Santa Claus was seen. Did you lose anything really? You had a fantasy of Santa Claus, but what did you have really? Letting go makes it sound like a big struggle, but what is it you have to let go of? Just a lot of ideas.

* * *

It's funny that we think the mind is going to help us figure out how to become happier or enlightened, when the opposite is true. We're so busy listening to it that we miss what's here in the moment, which is the only place where life can be experienced. And the mind is so clever at convincing us that the moment is not "where it's at" but in some fantasy or idea. It is so ironic. What a funny Mystery this is!

It's easy to make the mind into the bad guy. The mind is not the problem but rather the mistaken idea that it can free us by figuring things out. If you make the mind the bad guy, then you are just beating up the mind with your mind, and you're still not in the moment!

Embracing the moment—diving into it with your whole being and saying yes to everything that shows up in it can be done even with the mind. When you find the mind frantically trying to figure things out, you just get curious about that: "Wow, look at that. What an amazing thing!" The mind goes a thousand miles a minute through a million variations of this moment. What is this expression of the Mystery we call the mind? It's like the Mystery on speed!

The point I want to make is that the mind doesn't have to be left out. It doesn't have to be stopped or obliterated—and it can't be. If you are no longer fighting the mind and its hyperactive, obsessive behaviors, then it is possible to become curious about what is aware of the mind. What are we referring to when we say "my mind"? What does *my* refer to? Or when we say "*I* have a mind"? Who or what is this I? And what is the mind, itself, this thing so like Curious George the monkey in the children's story, which never seems to rest and is always poking its nose into things and causing trouble?

The trouble is we think that the mind is who we are and that it has something important to tell us.

It's good to be clear that that is the only problem. The mind, itself, is not a problem. Monkeys are cute! Although you still might want to keep an eye on them so that they don't get into too much trouble.

And once in a while, it comes up with something useful.

And a lot of useless entertainment! The mind will never give you the whole picture, though. So who or what is this that has a mind?

The Self, that which is aware of all of it.

And what is that?
I don't know! The mind doesn't know.

You don't know, and yet it is here. Everyone has a sense of this, so it's not something that is hidden. *Who* has a mind?

The mind can't speak about it.

* * *

Do judgments and thoughts of better-than/worse-than still appear after awakening?

Those conditioned thoughts still appear, and they are recognized as just thoughts. When that happens, there is the possibility of meeting them with the same gratitude that you would thoughts of love. When you meet judgments with gratitude, they can become a doorway to the Mystery, to something not yet seen, rather than a sticky trap. When judgment is met with passion and gratitude, the judgment, itself, becomes an opening. I have no idea how that works—it's a complete mystery to me—but it never fails.

However, it doesn't work to do it half-heartedly—accepting the judgment in the hope that it will go away. You have to fall in love with it. Instead of wanting it to go away, you have to want it to stay because you are curious about it. How does it do that sticky thing? How does it create contraction? Of course, as soon as you bring curiosity to it, it loses its stickiness and instead becomes a doorway to the Mystery. Curiosity makes it possible for you to see beyond the disguise called "judgment" that the Mystery has temporarily taken on, and suddenly there you are in the Mystery.

Nothing Personal

What if even your strongest emotions aren't personal? Is anything personal? What if this experience we are having as a body and mind is more like a radio that receives things rather than creates or generates them? You need a radio to play the songs that are passing through this room now, right? All this experience is floating around, and this radio called "you" is playing these songs called desire, fear, love, envy. Even resistance is just one more song called "I want to turn off the radio." What if your internal experiences are not personal but more like something a musician recorded years ago that is being played now?

Even the love songs aren't personal. Even the very dramatic, very sad, very happy, or very romantic ones aren't personal. There is nothing wrong with them; they just aren't yours. You can still pay attention to them, but there is no reason to get invested in trying to change them or get them to stay around. Every song on the radio eventually ends—even "Bye-Bye Miss American Pie," which was 17 minutes long. It would go on and on, but eventually there would be another commercial.

A radio is a great metaphor because a radio isn't like a CD player, which you can program to play what you want it to play. What plays on the radio is not up to you. Sometimes, it is a happy song, sometimes it is a sad one, sometimes it is an inspiring one. The Mystery is so wise that it knows exactly what song to put on in this moment. It decides what song gets played, and once it has been played, you can't hang on to it. Just being present while it is being played is the best you can do. That is all you *can* do. Paradoxically, this recognition that everything that arises on this radio called "you" is impersonal makes it easier to pay attention to what is arising because, if it's not personal, there is no reason to hold back from it.

Another huge mystery is: What is aware of what's playing on this radio? Then, you can ask an even stranger question: Is there a boundary between what is aware of what's playing on the radio and what's playing on the radio? Is what is hearing the radio and experiencing all of the experiences actually separate from the experiences themselves? It turns out that the listener who is hearing these tunes is not separate from this Mystery. Rather, the songs are streaming forth out of the Mystery, and the listening is streaming forth out of the same Mystery. There is a huge ground, or Presence, in which everything happens. The surprise is that this ground is not a place of knowing but rather a place of open-eyed discovery. There is no knowing ahead of time what will be played; you just discover in the moment the next song comes on.

Knowing and Not Knowing

There are two kinds of knowing. One kind is the knowing from the past, which includes everything we have read or been told. We have all invested a lot of time and energy into trying to collect enough knowledge so that we will feel safe. We want such a solid knowing that no matter what life throws at us we will feel like we know what to do. That is the kind of knowing that I'm suggesting is often useless because life is always throwing something at you that is beyond your knowing.

There is another kind of knowing, which is much simpler and wiser, and that is the knowing of the moment—the Heart's knowing. There is a part of you that just knows. This knowing in the moment is present to what is actually coming at you from life. It's not a knowing beforehand but a knowing that arises to *meet* what is actually happening in the moment. It is just present to whatever is happening without the rigidity or preconceptions of the other kind of knowing. As soon as something new arises, it is present to that, and the past knowing becomes irrelevant. Whatever you knew a moment ago is no longer any good in *this* new moment. For example, anyone you think you know—you don't know them *now*. You might have many memories and ideas of what they are like, but to know them now you have to be really present to them now and have noticed that they have changed—because they have.

Being this present, rather than making you foolish, makes you wide awake and intelligent. You are present enough to know what is happening right now because you aren't holding on to a preconceived idea of what *is* happening. Another way of saying this is that you trust the *source* of knowing more than what you know. If you trust what you already know, it will endlessly lead you astray. That's when you find yourself walking into furniture because you didn't notice that someone moved it since you were last there.

The source of knowing is giving you everything you need to know right now. It may or may not be what you want to know or be similar to what you knew yesterday, but everything you need to know for *this* moment is right here. I'm not suggesting that the other kind of knowing is bad and that the best spiritual practice of all is a frontal lobotomy. I'm only suggesting that you trust this fresh, alive knowing that shows up in each moment more than what you know from the past. The only thing you can really know is what is true right now in this moment.

Most moments are pretty ordinary; so this wonderful, alive knowing is often very ordinary and not always profound. Sometimes it is profound, but that doesn't do you any good when, in the next moment, you have to balance your checkbook. Then, you have to surrender again to what is true in *this* moment, which may be that three plus four equals seven. If you're busy thinking "it's all One anyway, so I'll just put down one," you'll get in trouble with the bank.

The truth is that 99% of the time, you act out of this innate knowing: your body breathes out of this innate knowing. This innate wisdom doesn't ignore your memories and other knowledge; it just doesn't give them validity when the truth of the moment is in contradiction to them. When they are applicable, like the memory of how to get home when you are driving home, this innate wisdom draws on them.

One reason we turn away from this deeper knowing is that it feels like not knowing. When you are just *here* without any preconceptions or pre-conclusions, the experience feels like not knowing. In every moment, you step back into *now*, which is a place of not knowing, and then the knowing rises up to meet it. Right now, this innate wisdom is keeping you breathing, it is keeping the blood circulating throughout your whole body, it is keeping every cell in your body doing what it needs to do. These are simple knowings, but they are actually very profound. How does our body know how to do all of this?

So, which will you trust? Will you put your trust in all of your ideas and what you think you know or in that which has been running your life all along, which has always been enlightened—so enlightened that it blinks your eyes when they need to blink? Your wisest moments have been when you have been present to what was happening. When you are present to what is true, what to do becomes obvious. However, this requires trust because knowing doesn't show up until the moment, itself, shows up—they arrive together. You trust by just giving your attention to *what is* rather than to your ideas about what should be or what you would like to have happen or to trying to figure out what you will say and do ahead of time, which we do in hopes that there won't be any surprises.

The good news is that even before you trust this deeper knowing, it has been working perfectly all along. The difference is that when you trust it, when you surrender to it, you don't suffer anymore. When, instead, you pay attention to your ideas about how things should be or how you want things to happen, this innate wisdom still gets you where you need to be, but because you are so busy with your ideas about it, you suffer. The good news is that this innate wisdom is not something you add or something you do or something you need to master, it is who you are.

How do I know what to do?

When there is no interest in thoughts, then knowing appears mysteriously from somewhere other than the mind. Test this out yourself: find out what it is like to be present without all your investments, desires, and agendas. When you are present without those, knowing shows up, although you never know ahead of time what that knowing will be and where it will take you.

It's strange to discover what happens when you are just present to life without your personal agendas and investments. When there is no longer any investment in things being a certain way, then you are totally free; you are free of suffering. Every moment feels like you are stepping off a cliff—you are endlessly falling into the mysterious present. This place is very alive and real, and it is actually what's been happening your whole life. However, this might not be what your mind thinks Freedom looks like. If your mind thinks Freedom means getting to do whatever you want, you will be pleasantly surprised to discover how much freer it is to let everything happen the way it does naturally, whether that is the way "you" want it to be or not.

* * *

There are times when my mind says one thing and my feelings say another and my feet just go ahead and do something else. When I go with my feet, there's a feeling of "yes."

If you are on to the fact that someone is a pathological liar, you just stop paying attention to him. Your thoughts and feelings are pathological liars. Once you see this, you just stop paying attention to them, and then they aren't a problem anymore. This pulls the rug out from under the way you've run most of your life. We keep thinking that someday we will find a true feeling or understanding, and then we will be done; but there has never been a true feeling or understanding. There is nothing wrong with feelings and understandings; they just aren't big enough to contain the whole truth, and because of this, they are lies. One very artful form of lying is not telling the whole truth. Feelings and understandings are very artful ways of lying because they don't tell the whole truth.

So do you just stop worrying about it and follow your feet? How do you do that?

Any answer I give you is one of these understandings, and it will fall short. It might work the first time or the first ten times, but there will come a time when that understanding will be useless.

The problem comes in trying to use an understanding as a formula for life because an understanding is never the whole truth.

It's uncomfortable for the mind to not have any understanding. At some point, however, you just stop caring about this being uncomfortable because the mind has never been comfortable. Understanding is like any other addictive substance: you get a little bit and it makes you suffer even more—you become that much more hooked on it. Like any good alcoholic or junkie, you have to hit bottom—you have to have spent your last penny on understanding and found that, even then, it doesn't take away the suffering.

When you finally admit that you don't know anything, that's when you start paying attention. If you have no idea what is going on, you had better pay attention, right? Rather than trying to find the right idea or understanding, you are just *here* in the moment as all thoughts and understandings come and go. You just stay in this compassionate Presence that allows all of it and is curious about all of it.

* * *

I want to know why the Mystery is doing all of this. Understanding gives me a feeling of silence and vastness.

If I gave you a good answer for why all of this happens, and you experienced one of those feelings of vast silence, you'd probably try to go back to that answer again tomorrow. There is no problem with understanding or with these feelings, but the invitation is to go deeper—to find the *source* of these feelings. Is understanding the source or is it just something you have used to give yourself permission to feel the vast, silent spaciousness that is always here? We think this feeling of spaciousness comes from understanding or knowing, but I invite you to find out what happens when you just let yourself not know.

I don't exist anymore. There's just space.

Isn't that simpler than trying to understand it? Just go directly to the vast space.

So, why don't we all just space out if that is the point?

I would never suggest you stop there—that's what spacing out is. Spacing out is trying to stay permanently in the spaciousness, which you will never be able to do. If you try, in a couple of weeks, someone will come knocking on your door demanding the rent! Or you will go to the refrigerator and it will be empty.

Instead of trying to figure it all out or hang on to these good feelings, get curious: who or what is feeling spacious? What is present when you are feeling spacious *and* when you are feeling contracted? What is present when you understand something really clearly *and* when you are totally confused? What is present in both?

It is the same awareness, but one is clogged up.

Just check. Is there really any less awareness in this state you are calling "clogged up"? Ideas or feelings of being clogged up may be present, but there is still awareness of those, isn't there?

What's the big deal about awareness? It's a mystery, it's not visible, it's nothing.

This is just the surface of it. Is awareness here right now?

But what is here? Nothing. I don't know what awareness is.

That is a truthful answer. That is as far as your mind can take you. Instead of stopping at the blankness of the mind, try looking even deeper into this Mystery. What is this that is present in every state? What is even aware of the blankness of the mind in response to this question?

It's like a trickster, having a ball at my expense.

It's definitely at your expense. The joke is totally on "you."

It's like a jokester that is playing with form, but I'm not aware of it.

You say you are not aware of it, but if that were so, how could you be speaking about it now? Is there really a boundary between what you call "I," the one who is the butt of the joke, and the one who is playing the joke? Can you find this boundary in Awareness or is Awareness present in both?

No. There is no boundary.

We've all been on this spiritual path looking for answers, and the joke is that answers are not the point at all; the point is to have a blast with the questions. The point is not to hold back from the Mystery just because there is no final understanding. Along the way, incredible understandings come out of the Mystery, but the Mystery, itself, will remain a mystery.

So, it will always remain out of reach?

I wouldn't say that it is out of reach, but the mind can't grasp it. In the end, you have to be willing to go beyond recognizing it and even beyond experiencing it to *being* it. There is no little "me" separate from the Mystery. If you sincerely engage in this inquiry, you will discover that it all turns out to be Mystery.

* * *

So, understanding that we don't understand is true understanding?

By the time anything registers in your brain, it is old news. That is just the nature of knowing—it's about the past. So, that is not the place to go to for this aliveness. Not-knowing is the place where life happens. Not-knowing is here right now, isn't it? It's easy to circle around it, but every time you rest *here*, there it is. So, what is always present?

I don't know.

Yes, and when the mind touches this place of not-knowing, it concludes that that can't be enlightenment or the Truth; so we turn away from that and look, instead, for something we *can* know. What happens right now if you just don't know?

It's hard for me to accept.

Yes. When we come up against this, we want to do anything but admit or welcome this seemingly bottomless not-knowing.

Since it is always here, I just invite you to get familiar and curious about this "I don't know." It is much quieter to keep looking into "I don't know" than trying to figure it out with your mind. It's restful isn't it? It's restful to admit that you don't know. Just rest here for a while. Just notice how rich this "I don't know is," how mysterious it is, how much is falling away right now and how much is arising to take its place. But don't forget to rest; you don't have to go back to trying to figure it out.

Oneness and Many-ness

The reason we spend so much time in spiritual circles pointing to Oneness is that differences are so obvious, while Oneness is not. The fact that there is both Oneness and many-ness may seem like a paradox. The way beyond this paradox is to recognize that differences do not necessarily mean separateness. Two things can be different but not separate. An obvious example is your fingers. When you look at your fingers, you see that they are different and they even look separate if you don't look farther down to your palm. When you do look farther down, however, you realize your fingers are part of the same thing—your hand—and even beyond that, they are part of one body.

One of the illusions that traps us is that these bodies seem so separate; but this, too, is just a case of not having looked deeply enough. The trick is not to look with the mind because the mind is not the correct tool for this. The mind is really good at noticing differences—between this finger and that, between this body and that. You could say that this is part of its job description. It is perfectly designed for noticing differences, and it serves consciousness very well in that capacity.

Once that is seen, there is no problem because there is something else that does recognize the Oneness, and that is the Heart. Notice I didn't say "your" heart but "the" Heart. That's why it has no problem seeing the connectedness—because there is only one Heart. It *is* the Oneness. So, now there is no longer any contradiction. The differences are not a problem when their *source* is recognized as well.

Even though the mind can't get it, check to see if something else is present that innately knows the Truth. This is the Heart, that which already knows the Oneness. It is not hidden. It is here right now, this Oneness, this Heart—the source of the differences, the source of all the states, all the emotions, all the thoughts. What a surprise to find it right here!

* * *

What is the cause of separation? I went down to the beach yesterday and had the feeling of Oneness, but the minute I talked to someone, a wall went up and I felt separate.

What if neither the feeling of separateness nor the feeling of Oneness is a reliable indicator? What if these feelings are the wrong measuring device for whether or not separation is present? What if feelings are not that accurate? Right now, your leg feels separate from the floor. Feeling is an accurate tool for experiencing differences like this, but then we jump to the conclusion that this feeling means that your leg and the floor are separate.

Where I experience separation is when judgment comes in.

Now we're talking about a thought. What if thoughts are not a reliable indicator either? You started off by asking, What is the source of separation? What if the source of separation is just the mistaken idea that thoughts and feelings mean something?

What I'm doing is having a judgment about the judgment.

Yes. Those are just more thoughts. What if even those don't disturb the Oneness? Then, your thoughts and feelings are free to do what they do best—indicate differences. Distinctions can be useful, but if differences are interpreted as an absence of Oneness, that is a misunderstanding.

Once a thought is recognized as a thought, it doesn't have to go away because it doesn't touch that which is and always has been One. Separation is just a thought, and that is all it has ever been. When you realize that, then there is no problem even with that thought. Notice how very conditioned we are to focus on the thoughts, feelings, and sensations arising in the body/mind. That is where we check when someone asks us how we are. We scan either current thoughts and feelings and sensations or how they have been for the last three months or three days or whatever and report on them—they are our reference for how we are (who we are).

There is nothing wrong with thoughts, feelings, and sensations, but they are only partial truths. A feeling can never be a complete truth: you can't feel everything at once with one hand, for example. Feeling is not an adequate tool for taking in Oneness, and thought is not an adequate tool for knowing Oneness. Thoughts and feelings are only useful for what they are good at. Once you realize this, then they are no longer so important. That Oneness that we are speaking of, is it here right now, without referring to thoughts or feelings?

Well. I know what I'm supposed to say.

Yes. We all know what we are supposed to say! The thought that you know the right answer—what is that appearing in? You can't really know that, like you know the right answer, and yet it is here. You can't feel it completely, and yet it is here. Once it has been recognized that there is this huge Mystery within which everything is happening, then there is no problem with feeling only a part of it. You are no longer seeing this couch as separate from the Mystery but feeling the Mystery in its couch appearance or in this animated form as another human being or as a feeling or as a thought or judgment.

How does this Oneness show up in so many different forms? Not one of them is separate from it, no matter how different it is—and there are some pretty wild things in this ever-unfolding Mystery. They can even end up living next door! The Mystery seems to delight in differences. It extends itself outward into countless forms and doesn't even make two snowflakes alike. That is how into differences it is. Yet, when you look with your heart at any aspect of the Mystery rather than with your thoughts and feelings, you will discover the Oneness underlying all the differences. There is something more simple and direct than thoughts and feelings that knows the Oneness—without knowing it.

Let the Heart Be Your Guide

If you stop and notice, it is obvious that the mind is not such a reliable guide for what to do and how to run your life. If you have followed your thoughts at all, you will have discovered that they are a very poor compass. They spin you around and take you on all sorts of wild goose chases.

Feelings are a little deeper place to check and a little truer than thoughts, but if you are honest, you'll recognize that feelings are not very reliable guides either. There is nothing wrong with them; they just aren't a good compass because feelings point in all directions.

Even deeper than thoughts and feelings are desires. This is moving in the right direction. When you are honest about your desires, you are being more complete. But if you reflect on your experience, you will probably find that following your desires has not led to great results either. So, I invite you to look even deeper for a guide. Look even deeper than your thoughts, feelings, and desires.

What is being pointed at is that which cannot be known through the mind. In looking deeper than your thoughts, feelings, and desires, you leave behind any sense of knowing in the usual sense. The mind doesn't register what lies deeper, and yet it is possible to recognize a place of deeper knowing that can be called the Heart. This is a very vulnerable place, which is probably why we speak of it as Heart. It feels vulnerable because there is a sense of not knowing in advance what is coming; things happen spontaneously in surprising ways.

This not-knowing and sense of things not being fixed or static, is an indicator that you are in the Heart. Being in the Heart has a quality of being fresh and new in every moment. The invitation is to keep diving into this place that is more honest and true and where you know less and less. As you surrender to not-knowing, you allow more space for this wise and knowing guide called the Heart to speak to you. It can show you more clearly than your thoughts, feelings, and desires what is really happening and what is true about your situation.

PART 2

Getting to the Truth

truth is too simple for words
before thought gets tangled up in nouns and verbs
there is a wordless sound
a deep breathless sigh
of overwhelming relief
to find the end of fiction
in this ordinary
yet extraordinary moment
when words are recognized
>   *as words*
and truth is recognized
>   *as everything else*

The Qualities of Truth

Most of us base our decisions on what we know, how we feel, or what will feel good. We do what makes sense based on past experience or we do what feels right or what feels good. We look to our thoughts, feelings, and desires to guide our lives; and yet, if you are honest, it is obvious that they have never been satisfactory guides for life. You can't know the truth of any situation by referring to your thoughts, feelings, or desires or by what feels good because none of these reflects the whole truth of any situation and, in fact, they point in many directions at once. Any situation arouses many contradictory thoughts, feelings, and desires. Using them to guide your life is like using a compass that was never magnetized. You hold it up, and it points this way and that way. It doesn't do you any good. The truth of a situation can be discovered, however, by becoming aware of certain qualities of truth, which have nothing to do with what you think, how you feel, or what you want.

One quality, or indicator, of being aligned with the truth is that it expands your being. When something is true, it has an expansive effect on your consciousness. Your thoughts, feelings, and desires recede into the background, becoming less important and less personal, because the view has expanded to include more. Like a zoom lens that has backed up, there is more in your view than before. Being in touch with the truth brings you into alignment with your whole being, which puts the personal self and its desires in perspective.

Another quality, or indictor, of truth is that it relaxes and quiets your being. This can occur on all levels, including the body, the emotions, and the mind. When you tell the truth, your whole being relaxes, and with that comes a relative quieting of thoughts, feelings, and desires. Alignment with the truth brings acceptance and peace, which dissolves desires and the feelings they arouse and quiets the mind and its defenses.

Experiences of truth also have a realness and solidness about them because they happen when you are in touch with the present moment. As a result, they also have a heightened quality of perception, or clarity, to them. Only the now has the realness that satisfies. Everything else is like eating sweets—you're never satisfied; you're always going back for more. So, another quality of experiences of truth is that they are deeply satisfying. They nourish you. Nevertheless, the truth doesn't always feel good; it can be painful and uncomfortable, and it may not coincide with what you want. Because the truth stretches you and your perceptions, it can be challenging.

Anything that is not true—such as most of our thoughts, feelings, and desires—can be recognized by the opposite qualities. While truth will cause a relaxation of your being and an expansion and opening up of your perceptions and heart, something that is not true will be experienced as contraction: you will experience tension in your body, hardening in your heart, a narrowing of attention, and a lack of clarity of perception. For example, when your orientation is on a desire, your awareness becomes narrowly focused on what you want, and you experience, tension, effort, struggle, restlessness, and dissatisfaction. Your mind goes a mile a minute, as it busily tries to figure out how to get what you want; meanwhile, your emotions churn in anticipation of getting or not getting it. Rather than things becoming quieter inside, they become noisier. Furthermore, being so narrowly focused on your desire prevents you from seeing the whole truth about it.

Because something that is true is experienced so differently from something that is not true, you can use this to determine if you are oriented toward the truth or not. Anything can be put to this test. If a thought, feeling, or impulse has the qualities of something that is true, then you can trust that it comes from your deeper being. If it doesn't have these qualities, then following it will not bring satisfaction but suffering.

The great thing about the truth is that it is very low maintenance. Lies are what require our effort and struggle.

However, the truth is completely spontaneous and unpredictable, and it might very well demand everything. Once you start using these qualities to orient your life, there is no telling what will happen. In some cases, the truth will wipe the slate clean and change your life radically. In other cases, your life structures won't need to change at all. Only what is true will remain, and you have no say about what remains and what goes. Find out what happens when you orient yourself toward the truth.

Desire

Desire is to a large extent behind our thoughts and feelings. It is what drives thinking and generates our feelings. Generally, our desires, like our thoughts and feelings, are not good indictors of what is true, that is, what will give us satisfaction. In fact, satisfaction of our desires usually only leads to more desires. We usually deal with a desire by trying to satisfy it in order to get some relief from the discomfort of desiring, but those doses of satisfaction only stir the flame of desire: You get a little bit of what you want and you want even more. The experience of desiring is always an experience of dissatisfaction.

Desiring never satisfies because it is an unreal experience. It doesn't have the realness or solidity of truth because desiring is not oriented in the present moment. The object of desire is always something that is not present in the moment (it doesn't make sense to desire something that is already here). A desire is always concerned with the past or the future, and no fantasy of the past or future will ever satisfy. If you were satisfied, you wouldn't be wanting anything. When your attention is focused on something that is not present, how can you be satisfied?

When this narrowing of awareness called desiring is occurring, what we are conscious of is the *object* of desire. We are not conscious in that moment of the *experience* of desiring. All of the qualities of a lie are rampant in our *experience* of desiring, but our attention isn't on them. Our attention is on what we want. We are so sure that that will put an end to our suffering. However, as soon as we include in our awareness the experience of desiring, we see that that experience stinks—it's no fun. It becomes obvious that desiring is the cause of suffering, not the absence of the desired object.

Just being present to what a lousy experience desiring is takes you beyond it because you are conscious of the suffering and desperation involved in desiring. When you are burning with desire and you become aware of that burning, the burning burns itself up. You don't have to talk yourself out of wanting what you want; just experience wanting it, and that will set you free of that desire.

Why does the movement of desire keep happening?

It's totally impersonal. It's just part of the unfolding.

There's a freedom if you recognize the lie.

Yes. Then, the desire doesn't ever have to go away. Freedom from desiring comes before the absence of desiring. Eventually the desire naturally gets quieter and quieter. If someone was present who you knew was a pathological liar, you wouldn't pay attention to him, and eventually he would become quieter. Desires are like that. They quiet down when you stop paying so much attention to them.

Isn't an essential part of the lie of desire that you think this thing will make you happy? The problem is thinking that you have to have something to be happy. That's a lie.

If you don't fall for the lie that getting what you desire will make you happy, then it doesn't matter if you get it or not. There's a freedom in that, isn't there? You can play much more freely when it doesn't matter anymore if you win.

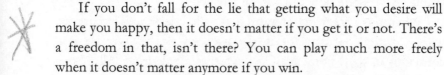

There are two ways that desiring can be recognized as a lie. One is if you never get what you want and the other is if you do. When you do get what you want, you realize that it's not the source of happiness. Even if it does make you happy, that happiness doesn't last, so that little bit of happiness only stirs up an addiction for more. Every time you get what you want, you just want more. And if, instead, you never get what you want, that fantasy eventually wears itself out, as you become exhausted by the suffering of desiring.

* * *

It seems like what you're saying is that the ideal is to no longer desire. Isn't there a danger in that?

What I am inviting you to do is really experience your desires, because it's not up to you whether you have them or not. Find out what is true about them. Get intensely curious about desire itself—not the object of your desire—but the actual experience. What is this thing we call desire? Does it have the qualities of truth or of a lie? And what does that mean if every time you look at one of your desires, it turns out to be a lie? It means you have to look deeper for the truth. Fortunately, all of your desires have been a complete failure at blocking the truth. The truth of this moment is always still present.

When a desire arises, if that is the only thing you notice and the only thing you are willing to admit to being present, then you are telling yourself a lie. One of the simplest ways of recognizing that your desires are partial truths is to notice that you have opposite desires. For example, you want lots of things and you want a simple life. Having both of these desires is not a problem if you are honest about having both of those desires. When you are honest about both, those desires become irrelevant. It's like coming to a signpost with two signs for Denver, one pointing one way and the other pointing the other way: both signs become irrelevant. They do you absolutely no good. If you admit to your opposite desires, then you come to see that your desires are irrelevant because you want something that is impossible.

* * *

Why do we desire things to be nice and fair when they are not?

Are any of these desires present right now?

Yes.

First of all, just let yourself experience these desires because the only place you can find the answer to this question is in the desires themselves. You won't be able to figure out the answer with your mind. To know the truth about desire, you have to look into the desire itself—not in your thoughts about it. Experience the desire itself, not in an attempt to fix it, but just the way it is. Until you find out for yourself what desire is made of, it will run your life and it will ruin your life. We're always so busy trying to get rid of the discomfort of desiring by repressing it or satisfying it. What if you finally just experience desire? Find out what your desires really are. Whose desires are they? Where do they come from? Just do it for a moment. What happens when you look into that desire and let it be there and let it pull you?

Sadness.

Good. Just stay with that pull. Let it rip everything apart because that is what desire does. Whenever you are desiring, you feel pulled apart. What happens when you let yourself be pulled apart?

I'd like to get rid of them.

Have you ever succeeded in all these years? What would it be like to stop battling the fact that your desires are tearing you up inside? Until you find out for yourself what desire really is, it will keep hurting you. But it can only hurt you if you move away from it. What is really going on inside your being when you are desiring?

Spiritual Longing

Underneath all of your desires is a truer desire—the longing for the truth, the longing to be free. This realization can be profoundly liberating because it makes all other desires irrelevant. Getting what you want no longer matters as much as truth. Whether you are comfortable or uncomfortable in the moment no longer matters because what matters is the truth. What matters is Oneness. What matters is going home to your Self. However, even this truest longing is a place of no rest. Longing for the truth can be a profound fire that burns away all the other desires, but fundamentally it is the same lie dressed up in spiritual clothing. Longing for Oneness is based on the lie of separation, that you are not already Oneness itself.

If you continue to focus on the object of your longing (Oneness, liberation, enlightenment) rather than on the experience of longing, you will suffer just as much as those who suffer over more superficial things. Just ask any spiritual seeker. You can go for a long time keeping the object of your desire— enlightenment—the center of your story. It's a much better story than being a crass materialist and much more liberating, but at some point you have to be willing to see that even that lofty desire makes your being contract. Even that never satisfies. Even that turns into an addiction: You get a momentary fix of Oneness, and the next morning you wake up and want Oneness even more. The desire for Oneness or enlightenment feels like every other desire. The question is: Are you willing to go deeper in this moment?

You are only free when you see that wanting the truth is as hopeless as every other desire. Even with this truest longing, if you give your attention to the object of longing and not to the experience of longing, you will suffer. But when you give yourself to the actual experience of longing, that longing opens up and quiets down, and you experience peace—the truth of your being.

Uncovering the Lie of Identity

Many people are not even conscious that they have a self-image. Or if they are, their attention is on how their self-image is doing and how they can improve it, not on the *experience* of having a self-image and how much work and what a pain that is. A self-image is a pain whether it's a horrible one or a great one. Either way, it is very high maintenance: if it is a horrible one, God knows, you have a lot to work on; and if it is a great one, you have to strive to keep every chink filled in so that no one sees through it.

If you shift the focus just slightly from how your self-image is doing—which is never good enough—to the *experience* of trying to maintain your self-image, what qualities does that experience have? Is the experience of giving so much attention to how you appear ever a place of rest? Or is it a place of effort and dissatisfaction? If you look, you will also see that the self-image is always about the future or the past. You are either trying to clean up what didn't come off so well or looking for ways to make your self-image better. You are far from the experience of the present moment.

Beyond using the truth as a guide for living each moment, you can go even deeper with this simple question—What is true?—and apply it to your self-image, your identity, your ego, your personality. These are all words that have been used to point to the aspect of your experience you call "me." What we're about here is discovering all the lies and, in particular, deconstructing the lie called "me." Your tool is this question, What is true?

There is no roadmap or formula for dismantling the "me." The holy grail for spiritual seekers is something equivalent to a big explosion, like blowing up the foundation of a high rise building with dynamite, which annihilates the whole building—the "me"—

in one fell swoop. That does happen. Some do go to the deepest levels of identity and experience such a big explosion of truth that the entire structure collapses, but this is very rare. There are many other possibilities for dismantling the "me" and no one right way. You can start on any floor of that building. Even if you go up on the roof with a hammer and crow bar and remove it piece by piece, the whole building will be affected, although less dramatically than dynamiting the foundation.

When you show up for work every day to dismantle this building, you get on this elevator, called life. This elevator doesn't have any buttons, so it takes you wherever it will. You may find yourself in the basement, at the foundation of your whole being, with a stick of dynamite in your hand, on the roof with a hammer in your hand, or anywhere in between. It's not up to you what part of the building is in front of you to dismantle.

The true joy is in uncovering the truth, or dismantling the "me;" so it really doesn't matter if this happens as a result of a big boom or whether every day you just go at whatever nail is in front of you and over time weaken the structure. I'm sharing this overview so that at whatever level you happen to be at, you say: "All right, this is as good a place as any. Here's a nail that needs pulling."

Is one ever done deconstructing?

The deconstruction takes on less and less of a sense that you are deconstructing "your" identity, "your" feelings, "your" thoughts, or "your" desires. Then, it doesn't matter whether what is arising is within "you" or within someone else. If the joy is in the deconstructing, then why would we want to be done with it? That's why I'm always pointing you to your own experience— because the joy, the liberation, the freedom is right here, right now. Putting liberation somewhere out there in the future is not deconstruction but reconstructing a new goal: a new, improved future "me."

Once you've seen through the lie of the self-image, you don't spend your day worrying about what "you" look like. You stop being concerned about whether your self- image is holding up. What fills in the emptiness that results is pure sensation. You experience a richness to the world that wasn't there before because there is no longer anything in the way of pure experience. You're just taking it all in.

Identity Formation

To see through the "me," you first have to take a good look at it and see what it is made of. When I ask you How are you? just notice right now what you refer to for the answer. How is this "you" that you call "me" doing? Do you refer to your thoughts in talking about "you"? Or do you refer more to your feelings or to your desires? After you've discovered the various places where you look to describe "you," just check to see if these thoughts, feelings, and desires have the qualities of something that is true. Do they bring relaxation and quieting of the mind? Are they deeply satisfying? Or are they accompanied by contraction, busy-ness, restlessness, and dissatisfaction?

When someone asks you how you are, and you tell them what you've been thinking about or what you think about something or how much or how little you have understood or learned lately, then probably a lot of your identity is formed around your mental processes. Or, if you go to your feelings to answer this question—have you been happy, sad, frustrated?—your identity or self-image may be formed more strongly around your emotional experience. We also try to form a "me" out of our desires. If that is the case, you are likely to describe how successful you have been in achieving your goals and getting what you want when asked how you are.

An identity can't be formed around a thought, a feeling, a desire, or an experience because these are constantly changing, often into the opposite thought, feeling, desire, or experience.

How can a thought ever be "you" if it is gone in the next moment? This attempt to form a "me" out of thoughts, feelings, and desires is like trying to make a sculpture out of clay that is too wet: you shape it, but when you take your hands away it goes back into a blob. No matter how many times you try, it goes back into a blob. The clay is just too wet, too fluid.

Despite the impossibility of forming an identity out of thought, we still try. Those who are identified with their capacity for thought believe that they are what they think. Consequently, they are very interested in what they think. It defines them. However, ideas and opinions are difficult things to pin an identity on because, whether we like it or not, like wet clay, they are constantly changing. This is something many writers can attest to who have written fervently about something, only to find that their ideas changed after the book was published.

Trying to form an identity out of an emotion is equally impossible, whether it is a good emotion or a bad one. We try to make a "me" out of an emotional experience, such as feeling depressed, by saying, "I am depressed," even though there are lots of moments when that does not apply. What happened to the depressed person in those moments? The same is true if, for example, you try to form an identity around "I am happy" or "I am loving." Then, you have a real problem when that happiness or those loving feelings slip away, as they eventually will.

Our desires are just as slippery as our thoughts and feelings and no easier to form an identity around. Nevertheless, we cling to them because they make us feel like somebody. Our desires give us some definition: I am somebody who wants a big house in the country, I am somebody who wants a family, I am somebody who wants to go to college. Having a want gives us a false sense of being real. We fool ourselves into thinking that we are some image of ourselves in the future. This image can never satisfy, however, because it is just a fantasy. It has no more solidity or truth than a photograph.

So far, we have been talking about identification with certain internal experiences—thoughts, feelings, and desires—but there is another place where identity forms, and that is with the body. Even when the other lies have been seen through, there may remain some identification with the experiences of the body—with the appearance of the body or with the sensations related to the body: how your clothes feel, the temperature of the air, the sounds hitting your ears, the light coming into your eyes, and so on. When there is still a sense of "I am the body," we may try to make this flow of sensation into a "me" and attempt to manage it by resisting certain sensations and grasping after others. And yet, the appearance and sensations of the body are also always changing.

Beyond the Self-Image

This attempt to form a self-image out of thoughts, feelings, desires, and sensations is a constant effort; you're never done sculpting this wet clay. Any self-image is there one minute and gone the next. You're never satisfied. You're never quiet. You can never rest. It turns out that the "me" has all the opposite qualities of truth. The "me" is a lie. We build this elaborate structure we call "me" out of what we think and feel and desire and sense, but it's all made up. Once you subtract all the lies, you end up with the truth, and what is left is nothing—emptiness. Underneath the self-image, there is nothing! When you are finally willing to admit to the emptiness beneath your self-image, it is such a relief! It's so real.

When we first land in this place of no self-image, it feels empty relative to the busy-ness and effort of identity formation, so we conclude that this can't be the truth—it's nothing. Besides, there is obviously nothing for "you" in this emptiness. So, we go back to our old ways—back to believing that our thoughts, feelings, and desires are who we are and that managing them correctly will make us happy. Many dip their toe in nothingness and freak out and run back to their more familiar reality. To the mind, even a lousy self-image can seem a lot better than nothing.

Often, just out of exhaustion with the self-image game, which can never be won, there comes a point when you not only recognize the emptiness but you allow it. You allow this nothingness at the core of your self-image. When you do this, you begin to experience the emptiness as it is, rather than your concept of it, and it turns out to have all the qualities of truth. When you allow that emptiness and stay in it, it becomes full with a truer experience of the world. When there is no self-image and no suit of armor in the way, sensory information flows very freely, and truth becomes obvious. Whatever is happening now registers right in the emptiness. Because your self-image is no longer monopolizing so much of your attention, your mind becomes more spacious and clear. You see everything more clearly.

Why is there so much fear and avoidance of that emptiness? We don't seem to go towards it naturally.

We are conditioned to think that what matters is having the *right* thoughts, feelings, desires, sensations, and identity. We've never been pointed to the truth but, instead, to these temporary satisfactions. With maturity, we realize that those things never satisfy. One of the things that causes an identity to finally collapse is having lots of the right experiences and accomplishments and discovering that those things don't really satisfy. And yet there are no mistakes. If the joy is in uncovering the truth, it first has to be covered up!

* * *

What makes you stay instead of run from this emptiness?

Eventually, the truth matters more than how it makes you feel. It matters more than the price.

It actually feels better anyhow.

It does, but maybe not initially. Initially, staying in the truth means that your false identity has to dissolve, and that may not be pleasant. But if you are willing to stay there, then something else fills the emptiness, and that something is everything! You realize that everything is you: this and this and this and this. There is a grace period in which seeing this truth is experienced as very blissful, but that blissfulness doesn't last either. It is just one of the side effects of this depth of seeing.

If the truth that everything is you has truly been seen, you are free. It's freeing to realize that, yes, that's me and that's me and that's me. And there is great joy in meeting yourself over and over again.

From Lies to Truth

One of the forms that the grasping and resistance we call ego takes is all or none thinking. One of the ways the ego tries to keep life under control is by coming to absolute conclusions. For example, if you don't get a particular job, you conclude that you will never get a job or maybe even that your life is ruined. Or if you get that job, you conclude that you are the greatest thing that ever happened on earth! These all or none conclusions can become very global.

The alternative isn't to stop doing that because that is just another conclusion—that all or none thinking is bad and must be stopped. Rather than going to battle with these conclusions, get really curious about them—What's true? If they arise, just look and see what is true. Get curious about the experience of these conclusions arising. What happens then is that some of the reality slips in. Instead of being entranced by the conclusion, you start to see that life is a mix of good and bad. There is something good about not getting a job and there is something bad about getting it.

There is good news along with any bad news and vice versa. Seeing the whole truth takes the sting out of these global conclusions.

The question is how much of the truth that slips through are you willing to look at in this moment? The more truth you are willing to look at, the less the suffering. Whenever you notice the bigger truth that surrounds and includes a conclusion, you won't suffer, and whenever you narrow your consciousness down to one conclusion, you will. The degree of your unconsciousness will determine the degree of your suffering, regardless of whether the conclusion is a positive one or a negative one. Even the conclusion that you are wonderful is a place of suffering, effort, and struggle. After all, if you've decided that you're God's gift to the world, you won't ever get to rest. Now you're responsible for the world!

Once there is an orientation towards truth—towards including *all* of your experience—you can't go back to the lies. The whole truth is the only thing that ever satisfies, and once there is a taste for it, there's no telling what it will swallow. It's like you've gotten a goat to keep the grass down in the yard, and one day you come home and the goat has eaten all the buds on your rose bushes. Then it goes on to other things. One day you come home and it's eaten everything: it's eaten your house, it's eaten your neighbor's house. You get out of your car and the goat is hungrily staring at you!

The truth is like that: once you've tasted it, there is no telling what it will swallow about your existence. Nevertheless, it is the only satisfaction, the only thing that nourishes, the only thing that is real. At some point you see that the truth is worth it—whatever it swallows. The good news is that most of the time it doesn't swallow your house. What it swallows is the idea that it is "your" house. It swallows the idea that it is "your" life. We think this is "my" house, and we draw a line around it. We think this is "my" body, and we draw a line around it. Truth comes and eats that line; it eats those boundaries.

To stay in that place of truth, you have to surrender all your thoughts, feelings, and desires. Any one of those will take you away from what is true. When you stay in that place of truth, there is no suffering. The truth might not always be what you want and it might not always feel good, but you won't be suffering anymore.

Surrender and Expanded Will

You know those bad new, good news jokes? The good news is that suffering can end; the bad news is the price. The price is that you have to surrender everything. There are no half-price sales. You can't wait until the season is over and then get your freedom for half price. You have to surrender everything. It's a very simple price scheme: if you surrender a lot, a lot of your suffering goes; and if you surrender a little, a little of it goes. But if you want all of your suffering to go, you have to surrender everything.

Many have the experience of an open, or expanded, mind, in which they are no longer troubled by thoughts because they see beyond the thoughts. And many also have an experience of an open, or expanded, heart, in which they are no longer troubled by emotional states because emotions no longer feel relevant in this expanded state. There is also an expansion of will that needs to take place, where your will becomes non-existent, and this expanded will—the will of the Divine—takes its place. If someone's consciousness expansion doesn't include this expansion of will, they can be very wise and very loving but only as long as they get their way. You can have great wisdom and compassion and still have a contracted personal will trying to run the show. The personal will can even co-opt the open heart and mind and use it to its own advantage.

This is useful in understanding what happens to many of us. We can be very expanded in our heart and mind but not in our will. Many experience a wonderful sense of being and then wonder why this often disappears. It is always a question of *how much* you have surrendered. How deep has that expansion gone? Have you let it take away your will, your desires? When your mind is expanded, thoughts no longer trouble you; when your heart is expanded, emotional states no longer trouble you; and when your will is gone and divine will has taken its place, then your personal desires no longer matter.

When people hear this, they often take this as a prescription and try to expand their will. You can see how trying to use the will to expand the will is a contradiction in terms. You won't ever get there through effort. The way to expand the will is simply to recognize that this expanded will, this divine will, is the only will that exists. There is no such thing as personal will. All your will has ever done is posture in opposition to divine will. Simply recognize that you are surrounded by divine will and that you've been out of bullets for a long time, so you might as well surrender.

You have already lost the war with divine will. In fact, you have never even won one battle.

Divine will is what is breathing your body right now. It's been living your whole life. The misunderstanding is that there is something separate called "my will," but all you have to do is look at your own life: Do you always get what you want? There are these things called desires that arise, but are they the determining force in the universe? It turns out that desires are not running the universe. There is something else also present that is much bigger than your desires, and that is divine will. It's not hard to see. All you have to do is look around, and whatever is happening, that's divine will. It's not hidden away; it's appearing in every event and action, even when you scratch your nose, laugh, or cry. Divine will knows what it is doing. Whatever you are experiencing right now is not a mistake.

In this simple recognition that divine will is here, your desires stop being relevant. They are still present, but they are held much more lightly. Once you see how irrelevant your desires are, it is possible to experience a different kind of happiness, one that is not dependent on getting what you want. You are happy when you get what you want and equally happy when you don't. That's how irrelevant your wants and desires can become.

PART 3

Being

every taste
every sensation
every possible pleasure
is already present
in the timeless
awareness
that is beating my heart
what use
in chasing dreams
that have already
come true

Transparency

The ultimate state is to become so transparent that everything that arises internally and everything that happens externally is met without any resistance or any holding on. Everything is allowed to be just the way it is without any judgment or effort to change it or hang on to it. Nothing is taken personally. Everything just flows easily from and through your being with nothing in the way, as if you were transparent. This quality of transparency is why we enjoy being around spiritual teachers. Whatever you say to them neither offends nor flatters them. Nothing sticks. Everything just passes through them freely. The same is true for whatever comes out of them: there is no blocking, censoring, or strategizing. It's a beautiful thing to be around that kind of transparency.

When we hear this, it usually stirs up some judgment and striving: Am I transparent enough? How can I be more transparent? We immediately try harder to be transparent. We turn it into something we have to achieve. But I'd like to suggest a simpler approach: just notice that everything is already transparent, not only your very being but everything you have ever put up to try to stop whatever is happening or whatever is arising from within you. All of your defenses and resistance have never worked. Whatever is happening happens anyway.

Not only are your defenses transparent but so are your ideas, ideals, conclusions, beliefs, doubts, and worries. They also are without substance. None of them has ever stopped anything. Take your conclusions, for example, your ideas about the way things are: I'll never find a mate, I'll never be enlightened, I won't ever do this or that. Have they ever kept life from happening the way it is happening? They are completely unreal. If your attention is on them, you may overlook what is real and true.

One of the favorite plots of science fiction is that the bad guys develop a technology or form of magic that allows them to create very realistic illusions. Then the good guys end up running away from or fighting these monsters, until at some point they figure out that the monsters aren't real. After that, they just walk through them and go about their business. It's possible to notice that all of your defenses, all of your thoughts, all of your feelings, and all of your desires are as illusory as these monsters. They are just as transparent. They haven't ever stopped anything. Even if we piled up all of the fears and desires of everyone in this room, we could still run right through them.

In case this transparency still isn't obvious, just look around you. Have you noticed how transparent everyone else is? It's not that hard to see past their defenses. Everything everyone else does to try to interfere with the moment doesn't work for them either. You have always seen everyone else and everyone else has always seen you. None of these disguises, or illusions, have ever been solid enough to block anything or fool anyone because they are only ideas. Nothing is really separating us. We are all transparent. You don't have to do anything to be transparent because there is nothing here that is not already transparent. Transparency isn't something you do; it is who you are—how you naturally are.

The price of seeing this is to admit that all your ideas and conclusions have been a complete failure at making you any safer or making things go your way. Occasionally things do go your way but not because of your ideas about how they should go. Your ideas and conclusions haven't changed the way things are happening.

Deep down, most of us recognize that we are imposters, that we are only pretending to be someone. We go to the trouble to create these illusory identities because we think it will get us something we want or keep away something we don't want. But even when it has worked, has the effort that has gone into creating the illusion of "me" been worth it? Has it ever satisfied? In comparison, do those moments when you are being honest and real and transparent satisfy? Does that transparency, that spaciousness of being, satisfy?

The first place we usually want to unmask the illusion is in our negative thoughts, but I invite you also to look at your positive ideas and ideals about, for example, what it means to be a good person or to be enlightened. Our positive illusions are very seductive because we think that having ideals is a good thing. Most people have ideals that they are attempting to live up to, like being loving or being strong or being beautiful or talented or unique. Everything they do is in service to these ideals, which are as empty as every other idea and have as much potential for suffering as every other idea. There is nothing wrong with ideals, but they are empty. They don't contain anything of real value.

If you've been caught up by one of these ideas or ideals, there is no harm done. Your ideas and ideals don't have to go away; you just need to see the truth about them. As long as there is a body, there will be lots of ideas, ideals, feelings, and desires; but at some point you recognize that they are empty and you stop taking them seriously. You don't lose sleep over them.

Once you see the transparency of these things, it is possible to shift your attention away from them and onto what is real. Then, your ideas, doubts, and fears pass right through you and so do the ideas doubts, and fears of others. You stop reacting to them. What once seemed so real no longer affects you because you see that they are actually without substance; they are transparent. This allows the truth of your being to shine through. There is no longer anything in the way of the expression of pure being. It is no longer clouded over by ideas, beliefs, conclusions, doubts, and fears.

You have never actually left this ultimate state we are calling transparency. You have never managed to make anything real out of nothing. You've tried, and it's been fun up to a point; but eventually you wear out this game, this idea that there is something wrong or that "you" need to change something.

My experience is that whenever there is a "me," there is non-transparency and resistance.

So, has your resistance been effective? Has everything you've resisted not happened? Do ideas, like the idea "me" or ideas about what is right and wrong, have any substance or does life just barge through your ideas about what should happen? What about this idea "me"?

It's a story.

What would that mean if all our ideas, including the idea "me" are transparent—nothing? If you shine a light on whatever is arising by asking What is a thought? What is a feeling? Who is this "me"? you see that none of them have substance. Thoughts, feelings, and desires have an effect, but they don't exist. Things that don't exist can have an effect. The invitation is to look and see if these things actually exist. As long as you believe something is real, it can affect you; but once you see it is not real, it won't affect you anymore.

Find out what is going on when you have a thought. Is it something you can believe? Is it something that satisfies? It doesn't matter if thoughts come; there is room in emptiness for everything. What is left when you see that everything is transparent, that none of your ideas, thoughts, or feelings are real? What is left when you stop trying to sell your lies?

Peace.

* * *

From this place of transparency, where does the effort come to work?

Where has the effort ever come from? If this thing called "you" is an imposter and has never existed, where has the effort come from up until now?

From my grasping, from my desire: "look at me and see what I can do."

And where did that come from?

Mom and Dad.

And where did they come from? Is there really something present that is here by mistake? Is there really anything present that doesn't have this quality of transparency? Is the essential quality of your beingness dependent on your having realized it?

No.

So, this empty, transparent beingness has been going to work your whole life. What would that mean if "you" never did anything, not even the imposter stuff, if it wasn't even "you" who had this problem of having an ego? Then, does the question of who is going to work tomorrow make any sense?

The purpose for suggesting that you notice that your thoughts are transparent is to get you to recognize that they also are made of this divine transparent substance. If they have this quality that we've all been seeking, then this is very convenient: thoughts are always available, feelings are always arising, and life is always unfolding in all of its glory and horror. What a handy thing it is to have this transparent beingness so readily available.

What I'm hearing you saying is that the same person is going to go to work tomorrow as yesterday but with a different perspective. Instead of believing my successes have been for this or for that, I can just find peace in it all and keep being successful.

Or not being successful. If everything is made up of this transparent beingness, then you stop trying to make an experience be a certain way. Once you see this, the effort to make any experience different than it is naturally falls away. If you see that neither success nor failure get in the way of beingness, then you are free. You are free to enjoy whatever comes—success or failure or anything in between. So, what is it like to be here without any guide and without any goal and without the need to avoid anything? What is it like to throw away whatever guide or compass you've been using and whatever ideas you've had about life and just experience the world without those?

Free. It makes the playing field bigger.

Yes. Nothing that happens can threaten this spiritual freedom. Just look: has anything ever diminished your freedom or has all of it been an expression of your freedom? There's room in this freedom for everything, not just success.

Nothing Special

The concepts about who we are create artificial boundaries between ourselves and the rest of the world. These boundaries aren't solid or real but permeable, like the border between two states. All of our concepts are like that; they create unreal boundaries. When you look closely at the boundaries, or distinctions, you've made between this and that, me and you, good and bad, enlightened and unenlightened, you discover that there isn't a line, or boundary, separating these things. What seem to be boundaries are a creation of the mind and language.

Once you see the unreality of those boundaries, what you lose is your specialness. Without a boundary, how do you contain the specialness? It leaks out. It's everywhere. You are no longer special because there is no boundary to contain "you." There is a lot of uniqueness, though. Everywhere you look is something unique. Every person here is unique but not special. No one here is more unique. When you are all unique, then how can that be special?

How much are you willing to let the implications of this truth sink in that nothing is special or has a higher value than anything else but, rather, everything is equally unique and equally sacred?

Does that imply having no preferences?

The recognition that nothing is more special than anything else doesn't depend on there being no preferences. It doesn't even depend on there being no attempt to make yourself special or to make your experience special. All it requires is the willingness to admit that you have never succeeded in making anything special. And if there is still a desire to be someone special or to have a special experience, just recognize that you will never succeed. You don't have to get rid of your preferences or even your desire for specialness; you just have to recognize that your preferences have nothing to do with who you really are and that specialness is an impossibility. Be honest. Be real.

The movement to draw boundaries, to conceptualize, or to create an identity by identifying with a thought, feeling, desire, or experience can only result in suffering because it is doomed to failure. We will never be able to hold on to any idea, identity, or experience because it will always change into something else. The true satisfaction is in seeing the truth, which simply means seeing things the way they really are—without boundaries.

Oneness Is Already Here

All of our suffering, all of our struggle, and all of our problems relate back to one simple misunderstanding: the belief that anything is separate from anything else and, particularly, the belief that we are separate entities. This misunderstanding results in our expending a tremendous amount of effort to reconnect to the Source. As part of that, we become absorbed in painful self-consciousness and self-reflection about how well we are doing. These efforts make sense only as long as we believe that there is an "I" or anything else separate from anything else.

The antidote to this simple misunderstanding is an *experience* of the Oneness of everything; just a belief in the idea that we are all one will not do. If that were enough, the whole world could be awakened with a bumper sticker that says: You are That! That's all it would take. But our ideas of Oneness will always fall short.

Words can only point toward the experience of Oneness; they can never contain it.

When people hear that the antidote is the experience of Oneness, they immediately wonder what they can do to have that experience: maybe if they went to India or meditated more. We go in search of our idea of Oneness. We think that Oneness is something different from what we experience every day.

The invitation is to look for this Oneness in ordinary day-to-day experience. What really happens, for instance, when you scratch your nose? Is there really a "me" that is doing that? Scratching your nose is actually a huge mystery. Nearly every muscle and cell in the body has to become involved to either accomplish this or compensate for this movement. Without this cooperation, you would fall over when you raised your hand. Scratching your nose is more the result of millions of cells cooperating than something "you" are doing. The reality is more like *we* scratch *our* nose.

It gets even weirder than that: scratching your nose isn't just something that takes place within you; it is part of something that is going on in the whole—you scratch your nose because someone in the room is wearing perfume or because someone just fluffed a pillow. Given this, it is more like the whole is scratching its nose rather than something "you" are doing. The whole is directly involved in everything that happens.

The same is true of every movement of the mind. Thinking doesn't just happen in the cells of the brain. Consider how many people had to be involved for a particular thought to be formed. Every thought you have involves everyone you have ever known: your teachers, your siblings, your parents, your parents' parents, your parents' teachers, and on and on. Without this participation from the whole, the thought wouldn't have come out the way it did. It wouldn't have the ground from which to form. You wouldn't even have the language to think with. So, not only do we the cells scratch our nose, but we the whole think our thoughts.

Feelings are no different. Every feeling also happens in every cell of your body. Subtle hormonal shifts happen with every feeling. Every twinge of fear, for example, happens throughout the body simultaneously in every cell. And, as with thoughts, every feeling you have ever had has been influenced by not only those you have known but those who have come before you. It is more accurate to say "we are afraid" than "I am afraid."

Everything happens more out of a "we" than a "me." Everything in the universe is involved with everything that happens. If everything in the universe participates in scratching your nose or having a thought or having a feeling, can you really call these experiences "yours?"

A recent study bore this out. It showed that anything that happened in one atom registered simultaneously in another atom regardless of how far apart they were. In fact, every event in every atom registers in every other atom in the universe. For this to happen, there must be only one atom, which has taken the form of many different atoms. Atoms are not separate entities after all.

Given this, astrology and all kinds of psychic phenomenon begin to make sense.

There was another wonderful study that filmed people having a conversation. They were able to slow the film down and observe what was happening in every instant. They discovered that those who were listening made very tiny movements when someone else was speaking that arose simultaneously with the speaking. Everything was happening at once; there wasn't enough time for the speaking to cause those movements. The speaker and the listener were doing it together. There was no separation between them. If you are really in tune with someone, you can often sense how the conversation is really coming out of both of you.

What does this mean? What if there is no separate "you" that scratches your nose or who has ever done anything? This idea of a separate person is just not true. "You" have never done anything, neither the most horrible things nor the most sublime. Even the idea of separation wasn't yours. It is the whole that has been playing this game through you. The whole needed a "you" for this lie of separation to be experienced. And yet, although "you" are not doing anything, in another sense you are doing it all because you *are* the whole.

You can discover this truth just by observing ordinary experience—any movement and any thought. Look for Oneness in your own present moment experience. Really look: Can you find a boundary between these words and your awareness of these words? Can you really find any separation in this moment? With each experience of Oneness, even a very small one, the tendency to see things as separate is weakened.

Suffering ends once the truth of non-separation has been seen because there is no longer any resistance to whatever is happening. Once you see that you are the whole, you lose interest in avoiding any experience or in having any particular experience. Whatever comes is fine, but there is no preference because you already are every experience. There is nothing missing, nothing lacking, nothing incomplete about the real you; it is already having every experience.

You don't long for anything because it doesn't make sense to long for something you already have. Nothing is missing because everything is you.

A friend and I were sitting around one day and idly talking, and she said: "Oh I wish I had Cindy Crawford's body." Then she paused a moment, sensing the Oneness, and said, "Wait a minute, I do have Cindy Crawford's body. I'm her too!" Once she took a good look at her actual experience and saw that there was no separation between Cindy Crawford and herself or between anything else and herself, it just didn't make sense to long to be a supermodel—she already was every supermodel on the planet! You already are all the money in the world. You already are all the love in the world. Longing for these things or anything else doesn't make sense once you see this.

When I say that there is no separation, I'm not talking about everything being the same. There are differences; there just is no separation. The Oneness expresses itself in many different ways, but it is all Oneness. The misunderstanding is that because things are so different, they must also be separate. You can look at your own hands to disprove this: your right and left hands are definitely different, but are they separate? Could your right hand exist without your left hand and everything in between?

I've been suffering a lot over the last two months. What you are saying is making me look more closely at my suffering.

What if it is not you who is suffering? What if it is not "your" suffering?

Yes. One thing I noticed about the suffering is there seems to be some investment in it.

In the same sense that it is not you scratching your nose, is it really your suffering?

It's just suffering.

Yes. It is just suffering. "Suffering is happening," like an itch happens, is very different from "I am suffering." And a whole different set of conclusions follows from "I am suffering" than from "suffering is happening." If "I am suffering," is a mistaken conclusion, then any conclusion that follows from that must be mistaken as well.

I see some kind of investment in holding onto my suffering.

The only way we get to exist as a separate entity is by having problems—by suffering. If it is seen that not even that suffering is ours, then where are we? What does that do to the "me?"

Exactly. There is an element of narcissism in suffering, as if I'm special because of it. And even that I have to let go of.

What if it is not even you who is wanting to be special? Once you see this, you realize you have been an utter fool every day of your life—but what if that hasn't been you either? The only thing that allows us to see this truth and not reject it is to also see that we haven't been doing any of it. So, what is left if the suffering is not yours and the reactions to the suffering aren't yours and the identification with it isn't something you are doing either? What remains when all these mistaken ideas are seen?

The river is left in which all of that is flowing.

Realizing that none of it is personal allows you to be really present to whatever is showing up, whether it is suffering or love. You don't turn away because you realize that it is all you. If your finger were bleeding, you wouldn't turn away from it and pretend it wasn't part of you, would you? If it is all you, you pay attention to all of it.

The point is not to separate from the suffering but to realize that the suffering is not separate from anything else—it isn't yours. Then there is no problem with it and no problem being present to it, and that is what heals it. Ultimately, when there is no mistaken idea that there is something separate that is being hurt by whatever is happening, the experience is no longer one of suffering.

* * *

My life has really been going great, but then I had two accidents within a week and I began to wonder if I was unconsciously trying to sabotage things.

What if it is not you who was causing your life to go great or the accidents to happen? You don't get the credit or the blame for how your life goes. It is all just coming out of the whole. It's the whole universe that is making everything happen, so it's kind of silly to take it personally. What if you just let whatever is happening be? It's crazy enough that we try to change the present, but trying to change the past is really crazy. Rather than try to figure out the past, just let it be.

When things are going well, the challenge is not to take it personally. We tend to take credit for things going well. But is it really you making these good things happen? When things are going well, the challenge is to remain conscious of the fact that it's not you doing the good things either. If you don't take the good things personally, self-sabotage has no reason to arise.

* * *

I felt some resentment toward someone who was employing me, so I told her and she reacted very strongly. Since then, my mind has been going crazy trying to figure it all out.

What if it isn't your mind? If it's not you that scratches your nose, it's not you that's been trying to figure it out either.
There was something in my interaction with her that is a pattern throughout my life.

What if that is true, and yet none of it is yours? What if it is just something that is arising and it's not personal? If it's not yours, then it's not up to you what shows up. Seeing this allows you to rest. The universe didn't create this experience by mistake. It wants this experience. The whole universe shifted and changed so that this experience would arise. It's just not *your* experience.

While this allows you to rest, there is also no reason to pull back from what is happening. You rest right *in* the midst of resentment. You get curious about it if that is what is arising in the moment. When you realize that you don't have to take her response personally, you can be even more present to it. In simply being present to our patterns, there is the possibility of moving outside of them.

* * *

Lately, I haven't wanted to deal with certain things that have come up, like fixing the water heater. The real issue is what happens when I have to deal with something I don't want to deal with.

This is an example of how feelings aren't a very good guide for what is true, because sometimes what is true in the moment is that you need to get the hot water working, whether it feels good or not.

What can help you to stop referring to your feelings and just deal with what is real is to realize that they aren't your feelings. They're just feelings. What would that mean if they weren't your feelings?

What came up first was that they are my mother's. There was an emotional pattern I may have picked up from her.

But that pattern wasn't hers either. What if it's not personal?

What comes up is personal preference: I don't want to take the time to do it.

Desires also are not a good guide. They exist, but they aren't a good guide. There is no problem with preferences as long as the truth is seen. Is it true that things should be easy? What's true is that some days are easy and others are not. The reason we keep referring back to *our* feelings and *our* preferences is because we think they are *ours* and therefore we have to do something about them. So, life becomes about trying to get the right feelings and trying to get our preferences met.

At some point, you realize the suffering in this and you realize that nothing you have ever done to make you free of feelings and preferences has ever worked. Feelings and preferences are here.

But what if you let go of the conclusion that a feeling is bad or good or that preferences have to be met?

* * *

My daughter has been so angry with me because I divorced her father. She is shutting me out of her life, but I want to still feel connected to her.

When you realize that the All is doing it all—your daughter's anger, your resistance to her anger, your desire for things to be different, and everything else in your life—you begin to see that what you want is not what determines what will happen. The All is not basing its choices on what you want. So now you can just be honest about it: there's what is and there's what you want. Are you only willing to see what you want or are you also willing to see what is?

So, there is all this rage directed at me by someone I love. There it is!

What's that like if you just let it be the way it is? It's okay if you want it to be different—just let that be the way it is too. Just let everything be the way it is, in part, because it's too late for it to be any different. It already is the way it is. For whatever reason, this is what this Oneness is doing now. The experience doesn't have to change at all for you to recognize that the Oneness is doing it all. This recognition alone tends to shift things.

* * *

I noticed that when you asked for questions there was a desire to express myself, and then this judgment came in about that. Something wants to block this expression.

It's not you doing either one. They happened.

It's interesting that you say this because I've always had the feeling that the part that is blocking is the lie, and I was judging that. The suffering lies in resisting that and wanting to get rid of that.

The antidote is not to go to battle with the lie but to realize that it is not you lying. You have never formed a judgment in your entire life. Lots of judgments have happened; you just aren't the liar.

It sounds like you're saying I'm taking responsibility for something that doesn't belong to me.

It can't belong to you. One thing that does happen—again, it's not you doing it—is that the lie snowballs into other lies. We go to battle with the lie and say to ourselves: I shouldn't be judging. I shouldn't believe that. I should be enlightened. I should see through all of that. I should . . . I should . . . I should . . . All of those lies follow from this one lie—that there is a "me" making this mistake.

The good news is that all you have to do is to see through that first lie for all the others to fall away. No matter how great your suffering is or how separate you feel from Presence, you are instantly back in Presence by just realizing that it is not you doing any of it. Then, where is the suffering? If it is Presence that is playing this game (let's see how much I can fool myself), then who is the victim?

We've been calling this idea of separation a misunderstanding, but there really have been no mistakes. This so-called misunderstanding is the only way that the Divine, the All, can have the experience of being human. It is the way this vast, untouchable you gets to be touched. It can't be touched unless it goes into the illusion of separation. Then, it can reach out and touch itself.

The Divine loves it all. It's all divine play. The realization that none of it is personal allows you to admit how much you have enjoyed it all. If you are having a strong emotion, all that is needed is to recognize how much you love it. The you that you really are is having a blast. What a ride! What an experience, for instance, to be vast, limitless Consciousness and be angry at getting cut off in traffic. Then, as with any game, Consciousness outgrows it and says, "Now let's see what it's like to get cut off in traffic *and* know that I'm vast, limitless Consciousness. Let's try that game."

This is very abstract to me.

Then notice how much love there is for everything.

I feel very confused right now.

Good. What a game! It's just not "your" confusion. What a great way to keep the game going! Just don't take it personally.
I have this desire to understand.

That's not yours either.

I don't get to keep any marbles?

It sounds like bad news to say that nothing is yours, but in a greater sense it is all yours—it is all you; it just doesn't belong to who you think of as "you."

* * *

I feel Presence and love, but I don't get the part about being all of it.

The first stage of awakening is the realization that there *is* Presence, there *is* God. This is a profound realization, but in that, there is still separation: there is a "me" and there is Presence. Many stop here and don't go any further, which is to realize that Presence is all there is, because if they did, they would have to give up "me." The price of admitting the truth is that "you" don't exist anymore. The final lie is the idea that there is a "me" that is separate from Presence. At some point, the truth becomes worth more than your existence.

* * *

How can we see that things are not separate?

What do you see as separate from you?
Everything outside my body.

What about awareness? Awareness is outside your body, right? So, is the awareness you have of my hand right now not you?

I don't know.

How do you see connections? You just look and see that you don't really know where you stop. Just look closely at the boundaries you assume exist and you will see the truth—that they don't exist. They are all a creation of the mind. Sometimes it helps to start with something really simple, like finding the boundary between you and your hand. Once this becomes obvious, try finding the boundary between what you call your awareness and someone else's.

They would seem to be different, but there is some common ground too. There are things we are both aware of.

If there *is* a boundary, it's a permeable one. So, what would that mean?

It would mean that it's not a real boundary.

* * *

What about the idea that we create our own reality?

Do we create it or are there just moments when we are precognizant? There is no way to distinguish the two; they would be experienced identically. In both cases, something is thought about now that gets expressed sometime in the future. What is really going on in those moments is a complete mystery. When we have a thought and it manifests, and we say "see, I created my reality," what really happened? Maybe future reality created that thought.

Nothingness

In addition to all of the thing-ness in the universe, there is also nothingness, emptiness, space, silence. This nothingness is as much a part of everything that is happening as the thingness. It is not separate. There are no boundaries between thing-ness and no thing-ness, between the sound and the silence, between the object and the space that the object is in. Everything is made of the same stuff.

If you go into an atom, which is a thing, what you find is mostly space. There is much more emptiness than thing-ness in an atom. And scientists can't even say for sure where an electron is at a particular time; they can only say that it is somewhere within a certain cloud of probabilities. Apparently, there is no boundary between thingness and no-thingness in an atom. Thingness and no-thingness are just dancing together at that level.

To bring this down to everyday experience: during a 30-day retreat, a friend of mine, while eating, came to see that an experience was inseparable from the absence of that experience. He realized that he hadn't really had a bite of food until he had swallowed it and every trace of flavor had disappeared. Only then was the experience complete because the absence of a bite of food—no-thingness—was inseparable from the experience of the bite of food.

Fortunately, you don't have to go on retreat to experience no-thingness, or emptiness. It's where every word I'm uttering ends up. It's where everything you have ever thought, felt, heard, tasted, seen, or experienced has gone. It has returned to emptiness. You can't taste no-thingness or see it or feel it. You can't in any way experience emptiness; and yet it is undeniable. This emptiness is

actually very alive. It's the source of everything. It is both where everything ends up and where everything comes from. It is the ground.

All of the things we try to identify with, such as our thoughts, feelings, desires, and experiences, return to emptiness. By the time any experience registers in your brain, it is already back in emptiness. Identification with these things is a lost cause. Dis-identifying with them is the only honest thing to do because they aren't here anymore. They can't be your identity because they're gone. If you think these things are who you are, then you will suffer when they disappear; but if you see that who you are is also the emptiness, you won't suffer when they return to emptiness.

The emptiness is also the space in which each new moment appears, and the only way something new can appear is for the old to disappear. The fullness depends on the emptiness and the emptying. The two can't be separated. It is just being honest, being real, to admit that everything comes and everything goes. The emptiness and the going are equally a part of the truth of your being as the thingness and the coming.

PART 4

The Mystery of Awareness

it is here
in the breath
it is here
in the stillness between breaths
    it is here
    in the active mind
    it is here
    in the resting mind
it is here
in the dream's panorama
it is here
in each moment of awakening
    it is here
    when all is well
    it is here
    when fear has nothing left to fear
even then
there is pure noticing
even then
there is no need for doing
    no frantic searching
    can find the obvious
    no seeking needed
    to find that which seeks
it is here
where it can never be lost
or found

Paying Attention

Before any words, there is something here, something present, something paying attention. It is very ordinary in the sense that it is happening all the time. It is the spacious Awareness in which everything happens. It's just nice to notice that during, after, and in between experiences, it is always here.

A lot comes into this spacious Awareness. Lots of sensations are coming in through your senses right now. Lots of thoughts are coming and going right now within this simple, ordinary Awareness. Then, beneath the sensations and thoughts is this movement within Awareness we call feelings, and deeper than that are desires.

None of these—sensations, thoughts, feelings, or desires—is a big enough container for this mysterious aware Presence that is here before, during, and after them. Because none of them is a big enough container for the truth of who you are, when you give them attention, they don't satisfy. Giving your attention or energy to them just creates a pull for something else because they are so incomplete. Whatever you have desired and gotten is soon followed by wanting the opposite. For example, have you ever wanted a relationship, and then when you got it, you wanted to be by yourself? This is only natural. Nothing we pursue through desire will ever be complete enough. It will never fulfill your deepest longing.

The invitation is to look beyond this ongoing flow of thoughts, feelings, and desires and to discover what is even truer than those. What is trustworthy? What is always present? What does not come and go? Because it has always been here, what you find turns out to be very ordinary and familiar—but a complete mystery. What is it that is hearing these words? What is it that is feeling the feelings? What is it that is desiring a relationship or distance from one or, more often, both at the same time? What is this mystery in which all of that happens?

When we are willing to look, what we find is something that can't be grasped with the mind. Just like you can't take a picture of a camera with a camera, this mystery underlying everything, including spiritual experiences, can't be found in the way you've found everything else. You can't ever get hold of it. At first, this can feel a little scary or disorienting. You're touching the Mystery and yet nothing is there. Your mind can't find any *thing* that it can describe or know, so the tendency is to go back to something more familiar, to something you do know.

In the end, it's actually a great relief to not know because it allows for the possibility of *being* that Awareness in every moment. Before anything is taken to be something or to mean something or to matter, there is this spacious Awareness. It has no boundaries or limits, and you can never be done exploring its depths and richness. Everything that appears in it is a beautiful reflection of it. I said you can't take a picture of a camera with a camera, but you *can* take a lot of beautiful pictures of other things with a camera. Sensations, thoughts, feelings, and experiences are all beautiful emanations from this that, in itself, cannot be experienced; but these expressions of it can be experienced, and each of them can be a doorway into the Mystery.

For me, this spaciousness seems to come and go.

Consciousness can become very narrowly focused sometimes, like when someone cuts you off in traffic or you drop a rock on your foot or your girlfriend tells you she wants to break up. What is lost when that happens?

Nothing.

That's right or you couldn't even tell me about the feeling of having lost something. What is it that noticed this narrowing of attention and can now tell me about it?

I feel like it's not okay to have lost the feeling of spaciousness. I judge it.

What is it that notices these judgments? What is it that is present even when judgment comes up? Does *that* ever come and go?

No.

No. Otherwise, you couldn't even tell me about it. That which is aware doesn't come and go. Once you realize that, then anything can become a doorway to the recognition of that Awareness.

There is nothing wrong with expanded states; they just aren't the whole truth. The whole truth is that Awareness also has the capacity for narrowing attention. You can't leave that out because suddenly you'll have to go to the bathroom, which is bound to narrow your attention. Then, what happened to the expanded state?

When you are honest, you see that, in spite of all the psychological and spiritual techniques you know, you don't have control over whether your consciousness is spacious or narrowly focused. The movement of consciousness between these two states just happens, and you don't know why. What happens when you just hang out here in not knowing—but looking. You don't know and yet everything is still happening. You don't know what I'm going to say or do next, do you? It's just happening. This place is very alive. It's not always grand and expanded and cosmic, but it's always alive.

So, then we just watch.

Right. This watching or noticing is natural. I challenge you to shut it off: stop being aware right now! Is this that notices everything an experience or is it who you are?

It's who I am.

Whether you are in an expanded state or not, is this that is hearing my words having fun?

Yes.

Even when the focus is very narrow, Awareness is having fun. It loves *all* of this. It loves the expanded experiences and the contracted ones. It's having a blast. That's what I mean about being more honest.

* * *

I have felt this feeling of peace and acceptance, of "great okay-ness," when the Mystery is touched, but only after a trauma.

That's often what breaks down our resistance.

Then, this can happen without all that? I have a belief that there has to be something to trigger it.

You believe that because that was true in the past. Just check: is any okay-ness here right now—even just a sliver, even just one thing that is okay right now? Just notice what happens if you give *that* your attention. You don't have to wait for it to show up as "great okay-ness"; this okay-ness is here all the time. It turns out that a lot is okay right now, right? Rather than referring to your thoughts, feelings, and desires, which are about what is not okay, go straight to okay-ness, even if there is only a sliver of it.

You don't have to wait for enlightenment; just notice the enlightened perspective—the okay-ness—that is here right now. This ordinary, everyday okay-ness is like the bass note, or drone, in Indian music; it underlies everything. It is wonderfully humbling to find out that what you've been trying to find, you are already drowning in.

Can this go away?

Let's find out. We don't want you to leave here with any remaining doubt. Can you find a place outside of *this*?

No

Where would it go? Have you ever spent some time getting a sliver out of your finger? When you were involved with that finger, for the moment at least, you probably didn't notice what was happening in the rest of your body, right? But when you were done, the rest of your body was still there. It didn't disappear just because you weren't aware of it.

So, it's all attention.

Yes, and this is really good news. No matter how interested you have gotten in some detail, you haven't diminished or harmed Awareness.

So, can I just be it?

Can you find a "you" that is separate from it? Has there ever been a "you"?

Just in the mind.

There has been an idea of a "you." There are lots of ideas in this Vastness. That doesn't make them real, does it?

I know the Mystery is always here, but I'm not always recognizing it.

Name something that you are paying attention to in one of these moments when you are not recognizing it.

The mind, the body.

Take the body: can you find a place where the body stops and the Mystery begins?

No.

So, have you ever been giving attention to anything else but the Mystery?

No, because there is nothing else. So, I don't have to worry about it! But you know what I mean.

Yes. So, now what? The best service you can give to the Mystery is to dive in even deeper. Get curious about it and don't stop just because it feels so complete and full. There is still the mystery of *this* new moment, of what is still undiscovered about it. That is the true service, and you'll never be done with that. Just check: is there more or less Mystery than there was last time you checked? Every moment there is more. Every moment, whole new levels of Mystery are revealed if you are willing to keep looking.

Telling the Truth

I'll try to keep it simple, and it is: what makes Self-realization, or awakening, possible is simply giving your attention to *what is.* Instead, we often give our attention to *what is not,* which is the definition of suffering. When I say "what is not," I'm referring to all your ideas, beliefs, opinions, concepts, desires, dreams, and fantasies. You don't desire something that *is*; a desire is focused on something that is not.

That's it. It is that simple. I could stop right here, and you could all go home, except that there are also some subtleties to this. One of them is that *what is* is always changing, so you are never done giving your attention to it. Another subtlety is that what I've just described as *what is not* is part of *what is*—because there *are* dreams, there *are* desires, there *are* thoughts. They *are* just as much as anything else is.

Another aspect of giving your attention to *what is*, is telling the whole truth about it. By this I mean telling the truth to yourself about it, not necessarily speaking it out loud. When you tell the truth, it has to be the complete truth because if you leave anything out, it is no longer the truth. All your dreams, desires, thoughts, concepts, fantasies, opinions, and beliefs are lies because they are not the whole truth. So, if you entertain them and don't acknowledge to yourself that they are lies, they can cause you to suffer. The good news it that just recognizing that they are lies frees you from suffering.

Let's take a simple desire like "I want love," which sounds very convincing. In the spirit of being willing to tell the whole truth, you have to question every aspect of that statement. Is it true that you lack love in this moment? Wanting love is based on believing you lack it. We only want things we think we don't have. To answer that, you have to look: is love present right now? Another part of that statement worth questioning is the idea of "I." Are you a limited container or something much vaster? In fact, are you love itself?

To tell the truth, you have to give your attention to *all* of what is. If a thought or desire arises, that's not a problem; you just don't limit your attention to that. You give your attention to *all* of what is, and then the thought or desire can't cause you to suffer.

The nature of consciousness is that sometimes it gives the Truth full attention and other times it retreats into the old ideas, desires, fantasies, and dreams—the familiar ground. There is nothing wrong with this; it just happens. Because you don't have a choice about what thoughts or desires arise, the only real choice you have is to either look even deeper into the Truth or look away. This choice is not something you do once and are done with but something you do again and again in every moment. Everyone in this room has had moments of surrendering to *what is* and then "lost it," gotten interested again in *what is not*. All you can do in that case is have compassion. This is just part of everyone's unfoldment.

This Vastness is experiencing itself through you. You are like its sense organ. You are what enables it to experience itself. In wanting to experience itself, it faced a dilemma: there is nothing that it is not. Since the Vastness has nowhere to go to find something that it is not, it creates it in illusion; and that gives it the experience of itself. It is so good at doing this that it even fools itself! At times, it is so deeply into this experience that it really seems like there is a "you" separate from this Vastness.

The invitation is to exercise the choice to tell the truth about *what is* as much as possible. It may not be that comfortable, but you will no longer suffer. There are not degrees of awakening as much as degrees of how present you are to the truth. The moment you tell the truth, you are free—there is no need to wait. You just have to tell the truth about *what is* in this moment, even if it is uncomfortable. The discomfort is not the source of suffering—but believing the lie is. Some think that all they want is to be comfortable, but that's not true. There is a huge industry dedicated to taking people to the top of Mt. Everest, and I can guarantee that when they're at 25,000 feet and their lungs are burning for lack of oxygen and the wind chill factor is 85 degrees below zero, they aren't comfortable; yet they report feeling more alive and present than ever. There is no lack of attention there because where they put their foot had better be the right spot. Give this moment that quality of attention—whatever is present.

You also have to be willing to admit to your happiness when happiness is *what is*. When you look at *what is*, sometimes you find happiness that is so intense that we call it bliss and ecstasy. Oddly enough, in our culture, we are often more comfortable admitting to our suffering than to our happiness, but to admit only to confusions or desires and not to the happiness that is always here is not telling the whole truth. I sometimes say that there are only two categories of people: those who admit that they are awake and those who haven't admitted it yet. You have to be willing to tell the whole truth—to be honest about everything that is present. Is there any happiness lacking in this mystery called Awareness? Can you really hold on to the lie "I want to be happier"? Can you really say that with a straight face?

Grace is the fact that the Truth never turns away from you, no matter how deeply or for how long you have gotten lost in one of these ideas, concepts, desires, beliefs, fantasies, or dreams—even the fantasy or dream of becoming enlightened. When you simply stop and look, the Truth is still present. It hasn't been broken, it hasn't been lost, it hasn't been taken away. It's here.

Again, the invitation is to set aside all your preferences about how *what is* should look or feel or sound and allow in how it does look and feel and sound—the particular disguise that the Mystery is appearing in right now—and tell yourself the truth. Is there anything lacking in this?

Being Present in the Present

Being in the moment means being present in the present. It's a funny thing to even have to talk about because you have never been anywhere else. There is no possibility of being anywhere else than in this moment. Every breath you have ever taken has been in the present moment. Every thought you have ever had has been in the present moment. Every experience has been in the present moment. That's who you are. You are that which is always present in every moment.

For some reason, being *fully* present in the awe and majesty of this moment and this moment and this moment is not as simple as it looks. Even though we are in this moment every moment, why aren't we always fully present to it? What gets in the way? The culprits seem to be thoughts and feelings, but if you look closer, what gets in the way of being fully present is something more subtle than the mere existence of thoughts and feelings. It is the nature of these body/minds to have thoughts and feelings and

sensations. If they were the problem, being more present would just be a matter of learning to quiet the mind.

Something else arises with this never-ending flow of thought and feeling and sensation, and that is *preference*. Preferences arise: you have a preference for one sensation over another, you have a preference for positive emotions over uncomfortable ones, you have a preference for profound thoughts over mundane or worrisome ones. When the Buddha said that desire is the cause of all suffering, he was speaking about preferences. Preference is just another word for desire, and preferences and desires are just another level of thought.

Why do we do it? Why do we want things to be different than they are, when that makes us so miserable? What is that in service to? Preferences and desires only make sense, only have a reason to exist, if another thought is also present: the thought "I," the thought "I am something." If I am this body, then it makes sense to have a preference for what sensations are occurring in it. If I am this particular bundle of thoughts and feelings, then it makes perfect sense to have these kinds of preferences. However, as long as you hold a belief in the idea "I am something," suffering is inevitable, since our preferences are only fulfilled a fraction of the time.

Many of you who have looked have already discovered that this "I" thought doesn't refer to anything. So, why are we willing to suffer endlessly in service to this imaginary "I"? We do it because the alternative is to be left with the experience of not knowing, to be left with the incredible mystery called this moment. Deciding that "I am this body" or "I am these feelings" is an attempt to bring the Mystery down to size, to make it into something manageable.

The alternative is hanging out with great big unanswerable questions such as: Who or what is aware of these thoughts and feelings? Who or what is having this experience? The alternative is to live in this place of not knowing. It just so happens that this is where Presence is found, where the present is found, where the whole truth of this moment is found, and also where aliveness lies. When we are not willing to live in the boundlessness of this question of who or what is experiencing, the aliveness of this moment is diminished. Trying to manage the Mystery like this takes the *life* out of life.

This place of not knowing is a very alive place. Everything you were searching for in your attempts to be somebody is already here right now in this Mystery. All of the aliveness and all of the love that you thought you had to do something to get are right here, and the price of admission is admitting that you don't know. Right this moment, you don't know where the love in your heart comes from. Right this moment, you don't even know where the thoughts in your mind come from. All that is required is to admit that there is a huge mystery at the core of your being and to not be fooled by the ideas, experiences, and possessions that you have tried to fill that mystery with, thinking that if you could just get enough of those, you wouldn't have to confront this place of not knowing.

Asking these unanswerable questions brings you to this moment where love is actually found, to this place where the beauty of the Mystery can be experienced fully. Then, there is no problem with thoughts or feelings or sensations or spiritual experiences or the lack of them. Then the possibility exists to not only explore this Mystery but live your life in service to it.

Just Say Yes

I've been inviting you to be fully present to whatever arises, to just stay *here* as everything comes and goes. Whether it is love or pain or joy or sadness, comfort or discomfort, understanding or confusion, you just say yes: "Yes, this too." In the moments when you don't know anything, you say yes. In the moments when you, through grace, know very clearly what you need to know, you say yes; and when that knowing no longer applies, you say yes to that, to the tendency for our knowings to leave. When deep states of consciousness appear, you say yes to them; and when they mysteriously disappear and you are back in identification—struggling and suffering—you say yes to that too. Whatever comes, you say yes to; and whatever goes, you say yes to. That is what frees up your energy to be here, to be present. It's that simple. My teacher, Neelam, used to say that if only this were more complicated, we would have figured it out a long time ago! It is really this simple: just be willing to say yes to everything.

I thought that things were appearing to teach me to see through the illusion, but if that were true, then why do the same things keep appearing?

If you have truly seen through the illusion, then it won't be a problem for you if something keeps coming back. It's like the illusion of water on the highway—a mirage. When you were a kid, you were so sure it was water; but eventually you learned that it was just an illusion and you stopped paying attention to it. You no longer mistook it for something real, and then it didn't matter that it kept appearing.

Do these things just go away?

Like houseguests, some just stop by and say "hi," and others you can't get rid of. Whatever is coming is coming to be recognized, so just be present to it. Then, its truth is revealed. If it goes, that's fine; and if it stays, that's fine too because you're not fooled by the illusion. You don't have to get rid of the illusion; you only have to see through it. The truth is that whatever is happening in your life is happening—it is already here. There is nothing you can do about *what is* right now. I challenge you to change this moment into something other than what it is. By the time you even come up with an idea, it is too late. The next moment is already here.

Can't you change this now with a choice?

It's obvious that you can't do anything about the past; but even with *now*, it is too late. It's too late now to change *now*, right? We play the same game with the future, thinking that if we can change the *now*, we can change the future—but we can't change the *now*. Even our ideas about the future are appearing in the *now*. Everything is always happening in the now. By the time the future gets here, it is already too late. It's *now* again.

Once we see this, it becomes clear that there is no doer: there is no doer because there is no time in which this so-called doer could do anything. Doing is just appearing in the now—it's just happening. Whatever is present right now is already here. Where it appears from and who or what puts it here is a mystery, but it is here. All of your wishes that this moment were different are lies because they aren't the truth about *what is* right now. That is why desires generate suffering. Desires assume that something could be different than it is, which is telling yourself a terrible lie.

* * *

My mind always wants to tell stories. I just had a taste of what it's like to not engage in that.

Yes. When you are engaged in a story, you're too occupied to be present to what is happening now.

So, not being engaged in stories is preferable?

Yes, and when the mind does engage in a story just be present to *that*. It's not up to you whether a thought appears in the mind. What is up to you is being present to that—just noticing how the story disengages you from the Truth. Notice the sense of separation that appears when you find yourself into your story or into a desire. You are cut off from something very alive and present and real, which leaves you with a feeling of longing or sadness. Just notice what happens when the mind engages in a story—even that is a complete mystery! What is it that is doing that? Who is deciding to have an illusion? Who is creating the illusion? Who is it that seems to enjoy them so much? You wouldn't go to all that trouble if there weren't some kind of payoff to illusion.

Being present is a very convenient form of spiritual practice: you don't need a cushion or a quiet room or a special book; you don't have to memorize any particular chants or postures; you don't have to eat certain foods or go to holy places. Being present works no matter what your posture or what you put in your mouth or what happens to appear in the mind, whether it is a greedy, mean thought or a profound, beautiful thought. It doesn't matter if you are waiting in line at a government agency or sitting on top of Arunachala, the mountain where Ramana lived.

This being present is always here. I challenge you to actually leave the present. Where would you go? Where is this other place than *now*? Despite all your efforts, you have been a glorious failure at leaving the present, so you might as well surrender and pay attention to it. It's not like you have a choice: "No thanks. I think I'll live in the past instead." If you find a way, send us a postcard!

* * *

It seems like you can't be in the present because it's not really there; it's already gone.

You can't be in the present with the mind. By the time something registers in the mind, it no longer is. The mind is a delayed recording device. But how limited is the present really? We somehow manage to fit the whole universe in there. How is that possible? There is something present in this very moment—this *now*—that is not limited by time, and that is Awareness. Can you find a time that Awareness doesn't contain? How would you even speak about it if it weren't present in Awareness?

If you are willing to play along with the Mystery, you are left with a wonderful sense of being on the edge of the known and a little beyond. This is a much more satisfying and alive place to be than in the mind.

The confusion you feel is really good news. What happens when you just say yes to confusion and hang out there? It's happening, so you might as well say yes to it. Normally, when the mind whirls and confusion appears, we run from it because it is uncomfortable. What happens, instead, if you say yes and stay there in this confusion? What is present even when the mind is whirling?

Awareness of the room.

Confusion comes and goes, but this Awareness remains. What is that?

It's a mystery.

There is no right or wrong answer to this question, but exploring this is very rich. Even as it recedes, there is awareness of it receding, so is it really receding? What are the qualities of this ever-present mystery called Awareness? Is it loving, is it curious, is it alive? What are its limits? What is its relationship to time?

Asking these questions can take you beyond the mind, but they can never take you beyond Awareness. After a while, in recognizing that, you become less fascinated with what is happening in the mind and more fascinated with what is happening in Awareness. The invitation is to get really curious about this Awareness that is always present. Nothing else is worthy of your trust or attention.

Love and Fear

There are basically two movements of consciousness: love and fear. Love is allowing *what is* and fear is resisting it. Those are the two possibilities in every moment. Compassion, wisdom, and peace are expressions of that allowing; while fear, doubt, cynicism, pride, and anger are ways of being in opposition to *what is*. When the mind hears this, it thinks: "Okay, now I know what to do. I'll just stop resisting what is," but that is just more resistance. Now you are resisting the resistance. Part of what has to be allowed is the resistance—the fear—that arises. Fortunately, this allowing is the nature of consciousness. It is what is happening most of the time. We allow most of the things in our world to be the way they are. So, it is a matter of noticing that this place of allowing, or love, is even big enough for fear.

All of your suffering is based on resisting *what is*, so it would seem to be the most obvious thing in the world to surrender it. However, it turns out not to be that easy because resisting is how we maintain our illusion of a separate self. It is what keeps that illusion going. Cynicism and doubt, for example, keep things at arms-length. They maintain a sense of self that is separate from this love that swallows everything. This love takes everything. The only way we can keep ourselves separate from it is by doubting or fearing it or by being cynical or proud.

Many of us are waiting for the Mystery to show up in a form that will sweep us off our feet before we surrender to it, just like we wait for the perfect lover. We tell ourselves, "I would commit to someone if the right person showed up." We think if we seek long enough, we'll find something worthy of our surrender. However, there has often been enough of a taste of the Truth to surrender to it—that's not what is missing. What's missing is the willingness to give up this separate identity.

What would it mean to live without fear or doubt or cynicism? Giving them up doesn't mean they never come back, because it's not up to you how much doubt, fear, cynicism, pride, or anger arise. They are the conditioning you inherited. What you give up is your allegiance or belief in them. Do you align yourself with them when they show up or with love and allowing? We think that our doubting mind keeps us safe from this Mystery, but our doubts have never protected us from this Mystery. It still goes about its business, and we are swept along. To surrender your fear, you have to give up this illusion of safety and protection.

Surrender is giving up the idea that "you" can do anything. So, even though it doesn't sound like much to give up your suffering and fear, it is the ultimate price to pay. The good news is that love does all the work, and you only have to be willing to meet fear and doubt when they arise. I'm not talking about surrendering to fear or doubt but being present to it and not so narrowly focused on it that you forget about the Love—this spacious allowing that even has room for fear.

* * *

Allowing is already here. If you look, you'll see that you are allowing a lot more things to be the way they are than not. You don't have a problem with most of what is present now. Do you have a problem with the sky being blue? There is a natural allowing going on, and it's not something you *do*. The nature of Awareness is that it takes everything in and loves it all. It loves blueness and pinkness and you-ness and me-ness. There is a natural love for itself, for all of its expressions.

Because the mind can only attend to one thing at a time, you can only have one problem at a time; the rest is just allowed. In the face of so much that is perfectly fine, how do we make that one thing that isn't the way we want it to be so big and important? And if that one problem isn't enough, we come up with fifty in a row. If that still isn't enough, we run through those fifty again. In this way, we build a huge case for suffering. But no matter how big a case we make, there is still a much larger universe of things that are perfectly fine just the way they are. The only thing to do with this tendency of the mind to resist *what is* is to love even this tendency when it arises.

The Death of Every Moment

Death is a wonderful and profound teacher. It shows up at various times in various forms, but I'd like to talk about a more subtle aspect of death. It is a death that is always here, that is showing up every moment—the death of *what is. What is,* is always dying, always falling away. It's replaced by what is now, but in the next moment it falls away again. This is a form of death that happens every single moment.

People who have studied physical death have observed several stages that people go through when faced with death: denial, bargaining, anger, grief, and finally acceptance and peace. Just as in confronting physical death, we go through those stages moment to moment, day in and day out over this day-to-day death of *what is*: our denial takes the form of trying to make whatever is be other than it is. If that denial is broken through, we bargain with God over *what is* or resist the truth of *what is,* which may take the form of anger or self-pity. Finally, we surrender to that truth, grieve, and accept life the way it is. These reactions don't necessarily follow this order, and several can be present at once.

All of these reactions—even acceptance—are in service to the mistaken idea that what falls away is who we are. We can never find a solid, secure place to pin this thing called "identity" on. To maintain a sense of identity, we deny the truth and pretend that things are the way they were a moment ago; and when denial is broken through, we bargain or kick and scream, which also gives us a sense of identity. If that doesn't work, we try grieving, hoping that if we are sad rather than angry, the universe will take pity on us and give us back a little bit of who we thought we were—a little bit of the life that just dissolved before our eyes.

Although nothing is the same from one moment to the next, there is enough of an illusion of continuity to maintain denial, resistance, and self-pity over the things that seem to be a worthwhile investment of identity: I am a therapist, I am happy, I am young, I am strong—all the things that sooner or later (and actually in every moment) fall away.

Acceptance is a necessary step and a big improvement over denial, bargaining, anger, grief, and self-pity. It is like saying: "Okay, I admit that nothing is the way it was, and I don't have a clue about who I am. How could I if nothing I know about myself is true any longer?" However, acceptance often has a ring of resignation to it, like saying "okay" but without passion or joy. Acceptance can feel like being beaten down: I'll let go since I have to.

Another possibility is to dive into this not-knowing and become passionately excited about watching things fall away: watching your body age, watching people change and move on, and ultimately watching your body leave life. Once you become excited about the fact that nothing stays the same, this truth is seen to be a great blessing. It is a huge relief to discover that you aren't all those things you thought you were. You realize that this ego/identity is not worth all the effort. There is a refreshing nakedness in not having an artificial self to maintain.

Embracing the death of every moment wipes the slate clean, making room for what is appearing now in life. What is it that is alive? What is alive is what is coming into being in this moment. When you finally embrace the going, there is also room to embrace the coming—and so much aliveness is revealed! Then, it becomes obvious what an illusion it is to identify with any of it and make that who you are.

Why wait until physical death to go beyond acceptance? Right now, go beyond acceptance to loving the absolute death and amazing creation in every moment. When that happens in the context of physical death, it can be very profound—when someone starts loving the fact that they are dying. In being in love with their own death, they fall in love with life—with the moments they do have. So, why wait until it's too late or your hand is forced by a doctor's diagnosis? Why wait to fall in love with *what is*—with constant death and fresh new life—when this place beyond denial, resistance, grief, and acceptance is available right now?

I should mention that even when we are completely loving the coming and going of everything, denial, resistance, grief, and acceptance still show up—possibly just as often—but they are included in this place of loving, which is big enough even for them. When they appear, you just love them and get fascinated by them and how it all works. Who or what is denying or resisting or grieving or accepting?

The Qualities of the Mystery

The Mystery, or the truth of who we are, is something that can't be put into words. All we can ever talk about are its qualities. To discover the Mystery's qualities, all you have to do is give it your attention. You don't have to tease it apart or break through to it; you just become fully present to it. Is there any lack of awareness in this Mystery? Awareness is one of its qualities. Is there any place where Awareness stops and something called "you" begins or is it all Awareness? Is it possible that this Mystery is not only not far away but actually looking out at itself through you— that it is closer than your breath? If you wanted to hide something, this would be the place because it is the last place you would think to look.

Another one of its qualities is its mysteriousness. It is a mystery that we will never solve. We don't know what it is. If you are trying to know the Mystery, then its unknowable-ness is very challenging, and one reason why many turn away from it.

Another quality of the Mystery is surprise. We never know how it will show up in any moment. Imagine what it would be like to meet every moment as the surprise that it is? Once you are relieved of the burden of trying to figure it out, what is left is just meeting this moment as the surprise that it is. Then, a natural arising of paying attention occurs, which is another quality of the

Mystery. It is always paying attention to itself. It has never stopped once.

One of the Mystery's most obvious qualities is that everything appearing in it happens all of a sudden. All of a sudden the phone rings, all of a sudden you feel sad, all of a sudden you wake up in the morning, all of a sudden you have the idea to go to a movie. Everything appears out of nowhere—from an itch, to a sneeze, to a moment of grace where your mind falls silent. Every thought, every sensation, every feeling, every experience has happened all of a sudden.

If you expect the Mystery to be predictable and consistent, then this quality of the Mystery will cause you to suffer; but if you surrender to the way it is, you can be present to it because your energy isn't going into resisting it. When you do that, the surprise is that this aspect of the Mystery becomes a great joy. Surrendering is a rather heroic word; it is really just admitting what is already true: you have already lost the battle. "You" aren't doing any of it.

The Mystery is always up to things we don't know about until we find out. All knowing is past tense. By the time our senses record it, it is already over. We're always the last to know. Realizing this does away with the need for a "me" to figure everything out and make things happen the "right" way, which is why we often turn away from the Mystery. What keeps us from surrendering to what is so obviously true is that we would have to admit there is no "me" after all.

We all have moments of not turning away from the Mystery, which we sometimes call "being in the flow." When you are in the flow and life happens so easily, it is obvious that "you" can't take credit for it. You didn't have to struggle and ponder and question and strategize. Everything just happened.

If you look, you can't find anything that would qualify as an individual source of thought or sensation or feeling. If you are honest about your own experience, you'll see that every thought, feeling, and sensation has just appeared all of a sudden. In one sense, the "I" is like a pimp: it stands around doing nothing and then tries to take all the credit. You can't actually find it. You can find endless examples of all-of-a-suddenness, but you can't find a form that is the source of everything. You can't find an "I" that can think up anything by itself. So, one thing that the Mystery is not is personal. It is not yours.

With this recognition that what you thought yourself to be doesn't exist, there is often a sense of falling into the unknown— of realizing that you don't know anything. You don't know what you thought you knew anymore. All your comfortable ideas fall away. You don't know what this all-of-a-suddenness is or what it is up to.

The invitation is to find out what is left when you let go of knowing everything you think you know. Dive into knowing less than you have ever known—less than you knew when you were born. Once you surrender to never finding who you are, then who you are becomes obvious. It's not found, it's not seen, it's not heard, it's not even something you can be aware of. It is just who you are. You are it.

You seem to be having fun. When did it start being fun?

Is fun present right now? When you go to the Mystery, is it having fun?

It's having fun and it's very enticing.

Could you let it have you?

Yes—a part of me is having fun.

When you check, is this Awareness that is having fun really limited to a part or is it having fun with it all?

It is having fun with it all.

So, why not just stay there!

That's the trick. How do you do it?

How did you do it just now?

By being aware of the possibility of fun being present.

Did you have to do anything or did you just have to look?

I looked and it showed itself.

What happens when you keep looking? Just try it. Just give it all of your attention.

Images appear.

Find out what happens if you keep giving your attention to that in which the images appear, to that which is having fun with all of the images, to that which is aware of all of the images and everything else that comes and goes.

Even war and death and fear and all of that?

There's room here for all of that.

Awareness has fun with all of that?

Fun is too limited a description of what it is having—joy, fun, richness, fullness . . . But, again, rather than talking about it, find out what happens when you stay engaged and fascinated with it— when you give the Mystery all of your attention every moment. Throughout your day, you can stay *here*, focused on *this*, not in some stale way but with an attitude of curiosity and amazement:

"Wow. Where does all this come from?" This is much more satisfying than any explanation of it.

Emptiness

The greater my awareness of Truth, the harder it is for me to find passion and enthusiasm in the world.

When you are willing to look deeply at the truth, there is often a point where everything else becomes meaningless and you can't find the passion you once had. You reach a place of emptiness where the old has fallen away and nothing makes sense or means anything anymore. A number of things might happen then: you might try even harder with your mind to make sense out of life; you might distract yourself from the emptiness by doing something exciting; or you might hang out in the emptiness, and then it takes on the quality of depression or apathy. Emptiness is another quality of the Mystery, which the mind interprets as blankness or nothingness.

There is another possibility, and that is to stay present to the emptiness and get curious about it. Apathy is the mind's reaction to emptiness because there's nothing in it for the mind. The mind can't go there. Get curious about the emptiness with your heart, not with your mind. When you come to the emptiness, the mind says, "This doesn't look right," so it turns away and looks somewhere else. Finally, there comes a time when you are willing to not turn away. You surrender to the deep recognition that everything you thought was important is empty; and yet, you don't stop there because if you do, it can degenerate into apathy and depression. What is present even in emptiness?

Peace.

Yes, and there is even more than that; and yet it's still empty because peace isn't a thing but a quality. Emptiness is the absence of things, yet it has quality and presence. There is something else in the emptiness that is so obvious that we don't even notice it: awareness. Even though there is nothing in the emptiness, there is still Awareness, or we wouldn't be able to talk about it.

What is Awareness? What is this ever-present quality of experience? It's a complete mystery, and yet it is always here, even when everything else falls away. All these amazing things come from what you have been calling Emptiness. How is that possible?

All thoughts and feelings and sensations arise from it. However, if you even slightly turn and chase after what arises from the Emptiness, you have turned your back on the source. We've all done that a lot. We've chased after things that seem like a good escape from the Emptiness, but none of them satisfy because they are only projections from the Emptiness. Like pictures projected on a movie screen, they are without substance. The invitation is to stay present to the *source* rather than to the appearances.

Another reason people turn and run from the Emptiness is that there is no "you" in it, or it wouldn't be empty. The only way to maintain the illusion of a "you" is by chasing after what arises from the Emptiness.

Awareness is a huge mystery, but it is not hidden. That is why seeking, searching, and striving never work. Would you think of seeking your hands? You'd never think of seeking something that is obviously present. Although you can't seek the Mystery, you *can* surrender to it. You can give it the quality of attention you would give a new lover because it deserves that. It is just as mysterious— in fact—much, much more.

* * *

I feel so separated and unwanted, like an alien. (tears)

Is it true?

No. (she laughs) I'm so angry.

Could you let yourself be really mad? It's not good enough to be a little angry; you have to be really fed up with the lies. What is the truth?

That I don't know what I'm doing here. (tears and anger)

That's the truth, isn't it? You just don't know. You get angry enough to finally admit that you don't know. It's a bum deal that this Mystery that is so rich and so true doesn't give you a formula. Then all that is left to do is pay attention; everything else is useless. This is that place of emptiness, where everything you thought you knew falls away. None of that makes sense anymore. So, here you are, with everything stripped away; and yet, what is present right now? What's left?

Just being.

Yes. All that is left to do is to be present and curious. One way of doing that is to look out at it all from the perspective of this pure being, or Presence. This body/mind is like a moving remote video camera. Through it, this Presence is getting a full reporting of what is going on. It's a very handy tool that allows Presence to experience itself. It created a body in order to have this sensory experience. This Presence is actually on both sides of what we're calling the remote video camera: it's both what is seeing and what is being seen. And what is even more amazing is that it is the camera too—it's also "you."

Once this Presence is recognized, the opportunity exists to look out from there rather than from the "me." When you do, the view is much more inclusive. Feelings arise, but they aren't a problem because so much more is happening than just feelings. Whatever is arising in the body/mind is only part of the whole picture. Sensations, thoughts, and feelings don't disappear; they are just seen from a new perspective, from that of pure being.

When I speak about being present and telling the truth, I'm speaking about being present to and truthful about the *whole* truth. Yes, there is a body that must be fed and clothed, rent to be paid, and other bodies to react to. Yes, all of that is often challenging, painful, and confusing, and at other times fun, interesting, and exciting. These things are true, but they're not the whole truth. So, the invitation is to look from the perspective of pure being, which is just a shift in perspective.

No matter how intensely difficult or pleasurable it gets from the perspective of "you," if you stay present to the sensations of contraction or grasping when they appear, you'll eventually become tired of them enough to stop. So, the next time something scary or exciting comes along, you just stay in the whole truth. You get to a point where neither something painful nor pleasurable is worth contracting over anymore.

These days when I begin to identify, the experience is like pulling on a pair of underwear that is too small. In the past, I would just put them on and say, "They're *my* underwear and *I'm* going to wear them." When I became more present to that experience, I could only get the underwear halfway up before I realized something was wrong and stopped. This old story "you" feels like clothing that is too tight. There is another possibility, and that is to be naked to this Truth. Maybe I should stop here; I may not want to get too much farther into this metaphor!

This Mystery can only be touched in this moment, and there are no formulas. That's why it feels naked: it's raw, it's present, it's alive, it's unknowable. In spite of that, you go there for the Truth, for answers, for motivation. It no longer makes sense to get more ill-fitting underwear or to embroider the ones you have. It no longer makes sense to get involved with clothes that no longer fit. When you stay present to this Emptiness, a lot of things fall away. Life gets swept clean. So much doesn't fit in anymore, but what is left is very rich, very true, and very real, unlike your old costumes.

PART 5

The End of Suffering

where is absence of desire
once I dreamed there would only be bliss
now I am in awe of the ordinary
now I am content with longing or no longing
desires do not disturb the source of all desire
life and death carry on as they always have
and always will
only the dreamer is gone
behind the flow of imagination
beyond any effort to be still
dancing in the ebb and flow of attention
more present than the breath
I find the origins of my illusions
only the dreamer is gone
                    the dream never ends

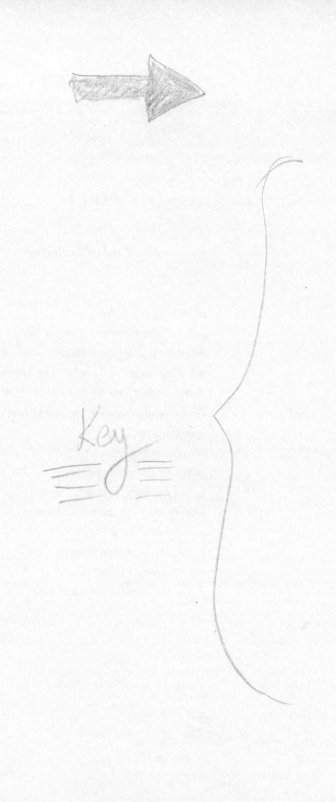

Key

Desiring What Is

Buddha said that desire is the root of all suffering. Desire is a very juicy word. It has to be if it has this much power. He didn't say *most* of the suffering or *much* of the suffering but *all* of it. Every single contraction of being is caused by desire. Because desire is such a powerful force, it is worth looking into.

One obvious thing about desire that often gets overlooked is that every desire is a lie. Every desire is based on the idea that things can be different than they are, and that is just not true. Things have never been different than they *are* in any moment. Things are always the way they are. You can see how this lie might come to be because things are always different than they *were*. Because things are always changing, we think we can decide how it will be next, which is another lie. Just look in your own experience: how often have things turned out the way you wanted them to? Unfortunately, every now and then it works and we get what we want, so we get hooked on desiring—like playing a slot machine. But, like a slot machine, it's a matter of random luck: if you play the game of desire enough, once in a while you will win.

When people see this lie, they become more accepting of the way things are. It's funny, though, their acceptance often has the quality of defeat or resignation: I'll accept it, but I don't have to like it! I invite you to consider another possibility. It's a strange possibility, but the results are wonderful, and that is to desire *what is*: meet *what is* with the same passion you may have had for *what could be* or *what should be*. Meet *what is* with that kind of passion, with the same force that is able to generate all the suffering in the world. Bring that force to bear on the truth instead of on a lie.

Gratitude is another word for this way of meeting *what is* in the moment. Gratitude is different than acceptance. Acceptance lacks passion and juice. That's why, even though people may see that things are the way they are, they often go back to the juice of wanting things to be different. At least desiring has drama, intensity, passion, and life—even if it does result in suffering. The other possibility is desiring *what is* wholeheartedly—truly saying yes to this moment exactly the way it is right now—bringing that kind of passion and aliveness to the way things are. This results in instant unlimited happiness because every desire for *what is* is always fulfilled!

The reason people don't make this choice to want *what is* is because it is so simple. Nothing is needed. People shy away from this because, in wanting *what is*, there isn't anything left for "you" to do. That is the price to be paid: to truly want *what is*, you have to give up the idea of being someone who can change *what is*. There is no longer a place for that. Changing anything would be working at cross-purposes to what you desire.

Then you come up against the inescapable paradox that even your desire for things to be different is something that you need to desire. You can't leave that out. You can't leave out the desires that arise—for a relationship or for money or for spiritual awakening or for the Truth. You have to meet them with the same gratitude.

Seeking the Truth is just another more subtle, sophisticated, dressed-up desire because the Truth is right here, right now—no seeking is required. The Truth has never been anywhere but right here, right now. People who are seeking the Truth are really seeking a better truth than the one that is here. The invitation is to meet even that seeking with gratitude. You have to want to seek the Truth if that is what is present, even though that seeking is based on the lie that Truth isn't already here. You still just open your arms and say yes to that seeking if it is present.

You are never done being grateful because *what is*, is always changing, always new. Every moment is a completely new chance to be grateful. Whatever is happening has never happened before: every emotion, thought, sensation, and experience arises completely fresh and new in the now. The opportunity to meet whatever is arising with gratitude and to passionately desire it, is always available. You never run out of things to be grateful for.

Something interesting happens when you desire *what is*: you begin to desire what will be. You find yourself naturally wanting what is going to happen next anyway. In desiring *what is*, you step into where it is going—you step into the flow, into this mysteriously unfolding, ever-new moment. This powerful force called desire can either cause all the suffering in the world or—when turned to right here, right now—become a power for being in the flow, for beingness.

One thing about flow is that sometimes the shortest path between two points is through hell, so that's the way the flow will go. So, if you think that being in the flow looks like a flat tire being fixed fast, you might discover that flow has a different idea about how long you'll be on the side of the highway and how late you'll be to your next appointment.

It's not up to you how many challenges arise in your life. This is devastating news to who you think you are. The good news is that it is up to something that is profoundly wise, something that can see that sometimes the shortest path between two points goes through hell—and sometimes through heaven. It has no preference for heaven or hell; it just sees where the unfoldment needs to go and doesn't hold back. That is what has been happening all along anyway. Has your life ever stopped unfolding in spite of how often it hasn't gone the way you wanted it to? It still goes, right? Something is steering it, unfolding it.

It is not some Truth "out there" that we need to be grateful for, some Truth that will show up sometime in the future. It's right here, right now—just the way everything is right now. Recognizing that whatever is, is only here for this moment and will never be exactly this way again gives us the passion to meet it with gratitude.

Often, the reason we don't dive in with gratitude in moments of suffering or pain is because we think that if we do, things will stay the same. We think that if we love this moment the way it is and all of its pain (if that is what is present), we will get stuck in the pain, when the opposite is true: only when we resist *what is* does it stick around. If, instead, we embrace the moment, it naturally unfolds into the next new experience.

It seems to make sense to go to battle with our conditioning because it is so obviously a lie and because it doesn't feel enlightened to have it; but fighting it makes it into something, as if it says something about who you really are. If you embrace it instead, you can see how ridiculous it is and laugh at it, and it loses its potency. It is no longer a problem; it no longer controls you. It arises and you say, "Great, wonderful, what a gas!" It never has a chance to turn into something called suffering. An event occurs, the conditioned reaction to it appears, and a complete enjoyment of both happens; so any possibility of suffering is immediately swallowed. We all are familiar with this process because it happens whenever something goes right. Every moment can be like this, where things show up, but nothing is a problem.

What cuts through suffering is simply choosing to love *what is* in every moment. It's not more complicated than that. You just meet whatever is arising with passion and gratitude, no matter how often it appears—because that isn't up to you. If it were, your old conditioning would have been done a long time ago, right? The invitation is to find out for yourself what happens when you are willing to waste your desire on *what is*. Don't take my word for it. For just this moment, meet whatever is present with a passionate embrace, and then see if you can find any suffering here.

The Nature of Desire

When you experience your desire just the way it is instead of your *idea* of it, you can be more present to it, and in being more present to it, you can experience the truth of it. When you allow yourself to experience your desire the way it is, you discover that every desire appears along with its opposite. Just reflect on your own experience for a moment. With everything you have ever wanted, has also been a desire to not get it. This is only natural in this world of duality, where everything has its advantages and disadvantages. Like every thought and feeling, this thing called desire is pretty confused: you want another bowl of ice cream and you don't want another bowl of ice cream. Whether you eat the ice cream or not, you suffer because you are stuck at this level of desire. George Bernard Shaw once noted that there are two great tragedies in life: one is not getting what you want and the other is getting what you want. This is the dilemma of hanging out at the level of desire: you're damned if you do and damned if you don't. Even if you succeed at getting your desire met, that stirs up the opposite one.

The other possibility is to let that be the way it is because that *is* the way it is—that is the nature of desire. It's not that your desiring mechanism is defective. The nature of this world is that it shows up in the form of duality. When you are willing to let your desires be hopeless, then the possibility exists of really experiencing them, of really noticing that desire is not a workable solution. Whenever you engage with a desire, it sets you up to suffer, whether or not it gets fulfilled. When you are finally present to this and honest about it, the futility of engaging in the dance of desire is revealed.

When you are that present to desire, it is possible to notice something other than desire that is also present, something truer: that which is aware of desire. That Awareness is like a light that shines on whatever you are aware of, including desire. This brightness is present right now, hearing these words and noticing the thoughts stirred up by them. Like a flashlight, it has no preferences or judgments about what it shines on. If you shine it on a pile of garbage, it lights up the pile of garbage; if you shine it on a work of art, it lights that up. Awareness has a limitless, freely-giving quality to it. It is willing to shine on everything because it is very wise. It isn't fooled: it knows that something beautiful is at the core of everything. It knows that the pile of garbage is its own self too.

Only when you allow everything—the internal piles of garbage and the internal works of art—can you also be present to this mystery called Awareness and let your heart be broken open by *everything* that is present. Desires are a lie because they are not the whole truth. If you only think that what you want is another bowl of ice cream, for instance, that's not the whole truth. When you allow desire to be here in its whole truth, the way it is and has always been, then more of the truth can be included. This is the movement of consciousness that ends suffering. It brings us to what is true and what is real.

It's not a mistake that desire is present. It is the doorway to a more complete view of the Truth when you are willing to allow it to be here just the way it is, including the opposite desire and that which lies beyond desires. Then it no longer matters whether a desire gets fulfilled or not, you just enjoy whatever the light of Awareness is shining on.

* * *

Why do I want intimacy and fear it at the same time? I've got a feeling that the answer is in the question.

The *truth* is in the question—that you desire and fear it at the same time. Once you admit one feeling, the other screams for attention. When you admit the fear and surrender to it, then the wanting cries out, "You can't give in to the fear—you *want* intimacy!"

And when you surrender to wanting intimacy, the fear nervously queries, "but what if you get it!" There is no end. If you are honest, you'll see that the same is true for every experience you have ever had: you have had the whole range of feelings about it. That is just the nature of feelings—they are contradictory. That's why feelings aren't the best place to look for the Truth. They will send you spinning between wanting and fearing. As long as the question is, How do I feel about this? you'll be caught, like a dog chasing its tail.

Why is also not a useful question. It's just a distraction. Let's pretend I could give you a really good answer. Then, what would be true the very next moment? That you still want intimacy and you still fear it. Any question that points you back to the Mystery is much more useful than asking *why*. Those questions can take many forms: What are these feelings appearing in? Does Awareness have a problem with fear or wanting? A very pure form of that question is, Who is it that is wanting or feeling? Who are you? By bringing these questions to the forefront, can you sense how the particulars of the feelings no longer matter? Even the contradictions of the feelings don't matter.

Those questions bring a lot of silence.

I invite you to go even deeper. This silence is a big relief, but there is still another wonderful question to ask: Who is it that is aware of the silence right now? The purpose is not to find an answer but to reveal another level. And then: Who is aware of this deeper level?

These questions we have just asked are different from all the others because the others have led you to knowing more and more, while these take you to knowing less and less, to letting go and leaving behind everything you know. Everything you know doesn't come close to explaining this Mystery.

The Ego

A very simple but useful definition for ego is the tendency to fixate, or grasp, either by trying to hold on to something that was here or by grasping after something that isn't here. What I am calling the ego is the movement within consciousness to do that. This tendency to grasp is the source of all suffering.

Notice that, according to this definition, your personality and innate preferences and tendencies are not the problem; the problem is grasping. So, for example, a preference for living in the country is not a problem as long as it is doesn't result in grasping. One of the forms grasping takes is identification: you identify with being someone who lives in the country. You think it is something you *are*, not just something you prefer; so, if you end up living in a city, you suffer because it doesn't match your idea of who you are.

The counterbalance to grasping is embracing. Embracing is resting in *what is*—just the way it is. Just rest in what is happening right now—what's going on in this room, in the mind, in the body— and just allow it to be exactly the way it is. Do you feel how the effort goes out of everything? Whatever subtle grasping was going on in trying to understand what I'm saying or trying to reconstruct your old ideas in light of this new information disappears. Do you see how that quiets down when you just rest?

However, by itself, resting can cross-over into the other kind of grasping I just mentioned—not wanting *what is* to change, which drains the life out of life because you end up living in what *was*, rather than *what is*, since *what is* is always changing. The counterbalance to this is curiosity, or paying attention to *what is*. To rest in *what is*, you have to pay attention to it because *what is* is always different from one moment to the next. This curiosity— this amazement—is actually very natural, very innate. What appears in every moment is pretty amazing.

Resting and curiosity are two sides of a coin: without curiosity, resting becomes lifeless; and without resting, you can't be curious about *what is* because you aren't paying attention to it as it is. So, if you find yourself wanting something to be other than it is, resting brings you back to *what is*; and if you are dragging your feet and not wanting an experience to fade, then curiosity allows you to become engaged in what is arising *now*.

Where it gets more subtle is that part of *what is* is the tendency to fixate—this boogey man called the ego. Ego arises. Every day something happens that we don't want or something doesn't happen that we wanted. There are blessed times when that movement away from *what is* doesn't arise for hours, days, weeks, months, or years; but when it does, the antidote is to meet it with resting and curiosity. The ego is just a confused part of consciousness that thinks it can hang on to things.

Then, there is the strange, paradoxical possibility of resting in ego, of embracing or falling in love with this poor confused ego. You just become totally infatuated with it and curious about it. You want to know everything it believes: "Oh look, it thinks it can get happiness from that. Isn't that cute!" This resting with curiosity and engagement is like resting with a lover: you get right up close and stay very present to it. Curiosity and resting are what allow the ego to be set free. They provide the environment for the confusion of the ego to evolve. You shine a light on the grasping, and the ego then sees that what it is grasping at is not the source of happiness.

If what happens to be arising is grasping, just for once, meet that poor confused ego with love—with an open, curious heart—and find out what is present within what we are calling ego. What is really doing this grasping?

Beyond the How and Why of Grasping

Some questions are better than others at freeing us from grasping. One question that weakens this tendency is How does grasping happen? Usually, grasping occurs in relationship to an idea. Our strongest grasping happens around the idea of identity— who we are. In fact, most grasping is in service to trying to have an identity. By grasping, we are trying to make something fixed. In this wild, ever-changing thing called life, we try to make something stationary.

When it comes to identity, we try to find something that we *are*, somewhere we can plant our flag and say, "This is me." The verb "to be" implies a stationary, fixed quality. For instance, "I am a radio show host" has a very different quality to it than "I host a radio show." The words "I am" imply that whatever follows is a fixed quality of being, not something that comes and goes.

We continually fail at this attempt to make something fixed. No matter where you plant this flag, the ground underneath it has moved, and the flag is no longer where it was. For instance, if your identity is "I am healthy," then a cold shows up. Life is endlessly shifting the ground under our feet. This futile attempt on the part of the mind to make everything fixed, especially this thing we call identity, is what causes suffering. However, just discovering this doesn't necessarily end suffering. Although seeing this diminishes the power of this tendency, this alone is usually not enough to end suffering.

Another way of diving into this mystery called suffering, called grasping, called "me," is to ask, Why is this happening? Asking this can bring you many profound insights. For instance, you may discover that your attempts at forming an identity are trying to compensate for not feeling connected to your mother or, in a broader sense, to the Mystery. However, even with these insights, you are still likely to find yourself grasping and suffering the very next moment that your identity is threatened. This question takes you no deeper than How? It doesn't pull the plug on suffering either. All you have done is taken the cover off the machine and seen how it is wired and how it works.

There is the possibility of asking a very different question: Who or what is grasping? Where is the grasping coming from? This goes right to the plug itself—to the source. When you ask this, you don't come up with intellectual insights. What you find is that who or what is doing this is a complete mystery. The answer to this is both profoundly unknowable and profoundly liberating.

This is the one question that can eliminate suffering because it cuts at the root of identity. What is found is that there is no ego. Another word for this grasping is ego, but when you ask, Who or what is the ego? you don't find anything. It's quite a surprise to find that grasping comes from the same mysterious source as everything else—there is no separate something called an ego that is doing it. Ego is just a description of the how and why; there isn't a who.

Asking how or why suffering happens is like standing at the edge of the Grand Canyon and being fascinated with a pebble at your feet. How and why questions take you in the direction of the suffering and identification but never beyond that to the incomprehensible Mystery that is doing it all. These questions give you a sense of control over the grasping. They help you manage it so that it doesn't turn into an addiction, or they direct the grasping toward more socially acceptable things or toward more spiritual things.

In the end, what is left is the more fundamental and unanswerable question, Who is grasping? You discover you can't even claim your suffering as your own. It isn't your ego doing it, because when you look, there is no such thing. You don't even know what suffering is anymore. It isn't what you assumed it to be—your problem—but something much more mysterious. You are left with the strange paradox that grasping comes from the same place as any joy or pleasure you can experience. Ego and God come from the same place. When you realize that ego and God are both expressions of the same thing, you don't know anymore what either of these are.

You are left with a huge sense of not knowing anything. The attempt to make something knowable out of the Mystery is useless. It doesn't accomplish anything. The pebble is actually as big a mystery as the Grand Canyon. It's as unknowable in its essence. In the recognition of the vastness of Being, the pebble— or ego— becomes relatively less important but no less divine or mysterious. It's just more of this divine mystery, not any more or any less special than anything else.

The only question, then, is how far are you willing to look— how far are you willing to raise your eyes from this pebble, this "me," to where it is coming from? Who is it that has this idea called "me"? Even if at first it overwhelms you, like looking at an endless Grand Canyon, and even if you can never be done exploring it, are you willing to look?

I feel frustration over losing the awakening I experienced last week.

When you see something equivalent to the Grand Canyon, you have to be willing to continue the inquiry. If you have the idea that now you can just stop and put up camp here, you'll suffer. That's the mind trying to plant the flag in the Grand Canyon. It's not about what is seen but about being willing to let go of whatever is seen and ask, Who or what is seeing it? When this is asked sincerely, you come up against this place of no seer, no thing-ness. Seeing is present, but there is no seer; and when there is no seer, there is no one to have a problem.

You need to keep asking the question and not stop when a nice experience arises. The question will point you beyond nice experiences to nothing—to no thing. We can stay in a nice experience, run back to a familiar one, or—and this is where the suffering ends—step into the nothing, into the not-knowing, into this moment. In this moment, there is nothing left from any experience you have ever had; it's all gone. There are no fixed qualities to this moment. There is nothing there for "you." There is not even a "you" for there to be something there for.

(Another questioner) *I feel some frustration because I've been to the place you're talking about, but I don't know how to get back there again.*

Good because you never can. Anywhere you have been is now ancient history. Right now, the opportunity is to find out who is feeling frustration. That is what you can experience right now because that is what is here right now. You can't experience who it is that once experienced this place we are talking about; but in this moment, frustration is a rich opportunity for inquiry.

It's me.

Who is that?

The part of me that is localized around this body.

What is the source of all the parts of "me"? (pause) This is good. You're looking and you can't find it.

I'm also feeling fear.

That's always a good sign. If there weren't some fear, it wouldn't be the Mystery you were touching on but some idea about it. Fear is a sign that you are looking into the unknown. Just stay in this not-knowing. Find out what is true about it. What is present even when you don't know?

What's present is something or someone that's looking.

Yes, looking is present even though not-knowing is present. There is still this mystery called looking. When you turn that looking back onto itself, you don't find a someone or a something; you just find looking. What are the qualities of this not-knowing? What is not-knowing like?

There's an "okayness"—and it is uncomfortable.

Fortunately, comfort is not the source of happiness nor will it bring an end suffering. There are lots of very comfortable people who are suffering deeply. It's just not good news for the mind to find out that the source of everything is something that it can never touch, never get a handle on, never control, never direct. *That's very disquieting.*

Just check in the Heart. Find out what its experience is of this very alive, never-the-same-way-twice Mystery. This uncomfortable not-knowing is as far as the mind will take you. To go further, you have to include more than the mind. Rest *here* in the Heart—not in something that comes out of the Mystery—but at the source. The

Heart is this resting. It would be nice if there were a place where frustration never shows up. In the meantime, rest here at the source of frustration because frustration, like bliss and everything else, comes and goes. Rest at the source of both the good and bad feelings. When you rest, you automatically drop deeper than feelings. They still arise, but you stop making the effort to feel less frustrated or to feel more blissful.

The frustration feels unpeaceful.

Are feelings a reliable guide?

Feelings are a signal to me that either my thinking is off or I'm out of alignment with reality.

Is that true? What if feelings weren't an indicator of alignment or a lack of it? What if feelings were not reliable indicators? It broadens the focus. If frustration is not a reliable indicator, then we need to look at something bigger than frustration. Then, what matters is not the fact that frustration is appearing but what it is appearing in.

(Another questioner) *What about habitual behaviors that cause suffering?*

If you get curious about a habit, you won't even be able to call it a habit anymore. When you get curious about the suffering in this moment, it won't be suffering anymore. We suffer over what is arising in the Mystery, but it has already changed. It's not even arising anymore. Yet somehow we can continue to fight with this thing that is not even happening anymore. Since the Mystery is always changing, anything you suffer over is already gone. If you get curious about the suffering, you won't be able to find the reason for it anymore. Suffering is just a concept, and what you are still suffering over is long gone. The Mystery has already moved on.

Then what is habit?

Even though the Mystery has moved on, we keep pushing the button that gave us the good feeling in the past. All pleasure and enjoyment are also in the past. The Mystery, here and now, is neither suffering nor experiencing pleasure. There is not enough time in the moment to suffer or to enjoy it. Those are things you do after some reflection on the moment. We take something that appears and make it into a concept and call it bad or wonderful. That is how we play this conceptual game called suffering or this conceptual game called enjoyment. We make up a story and tell it to ourselves, and who knows better than us how to tell a story that will hook us? We are all master storytellers. This is where it gets strange: where does the story come from? Who is it that is hypnotizing whom with this story?

Whenever your attention is taken by any story, there is suffering. Even the story "this is wonderful" is suffering disguised as enjoyment because whatever you said that about is already gone. When you stop trying to hang on to these ideas of "this is wonderful" or "this is bad," you find that you lose interest in them; you're just too busy being *here* to suffer.

What comes out of the Mystery is always perfect. It's exactly right for that moment. The Mystery is much better at figuring out what to do in the moment than your story is. Your story is too slow; it can't keep up with the moment. Eventually, you begin to trust the Mystery and get used to the fact that it happens to feel uncomfortable and disorienting. You realize that whatever shows up is just right, even if it is sometimes uncomfortable or difficult. (Another questioner) *Including the story?*

Yes, when you are willing to meet it as a story. It turns out that it was all perfect, even the wonderful play we call ego and suffering. When the story appeared, that was perfect. What about now, can you honestly say that the story is what is true right now? Can you say that anything you have ever known is true right now?

I don't know what is true.

That's good because when you don't know, you pay attention; and paying attention is very alive. When you think you know, you stop paying attention; but the truth is that you don't know. This is much more honest than any story. You begin to trust that the Mystery knows better than you what is supposed to appear right now, so you pay attention to what it knows. It's much wiser than anything you could know because anything you know is old—it's about what already happened, what was true before. That is all you can ever know, because in this moment, there is no time to form a thought about here and now. Thoughts are not relevant, feelings are not relevant, and desires are not relevant because by the time they register, they are no longer true.

What about a thought about the wall being white? The wall is not about to turn purple.

The wall isn't the same as when you had that thought. It's very yellow right now because of the light. With each flicker of the candle, it changes. Tomorrow morning, when the sun is rising, that wall could be pink; and when the lights are off, it has no color. What the eye registers from that wall is different in every moment; it's never the same. Your idea that the wall is white keeps you from noticing what your experience of the wall is right now. We never have the same experience twice, but our concepts often keep us from noticing this.

Words and concepts are useful when you need to go to the paint store for some off-white paint. For such practical things, words and concepts aren't a problem. The danger is that we can become addicted to having a concept for everything. When it comes to describing who we are, words and concepts are useless.

What's in It for Me?

We suffer because we have a misguided framework for life. The framework we have been conditioned to lead our life by is the question, What's in it for me or What's good for me? Even people on a spiritual path ask this question but in more spiritual terms: How can "I" be more spiritual? How can "I" have more spiritual experiences? How can "I" become enlightened? We use this question like a compass and go where it points, but it never points true; it takes us in circles. It can't take us where we really want to go.

The question What's good for me? is inherently flawed. One flaw is the idea that something is either good or bad. The nature of everything that has ever happened in this world of duality is both good *and* bad. Anything that seems good or bad has, at the same time, the opposite quality. A deeper flaw is the idea of "me." There is no "me," no container called "me" to hold the experience of good or bad.

The alternative is the question What is true? This is an accurate compass. It points right to the spot where you are already standing. For the illusory "me, which likes to take a journey or *do* something, this is not such an attractive compass. It doesn't want to be pointed to what is already here. However, when you have tried every possible way to make things better for "me," including spiritual means, you eventually wear out your fascination with these journeys, with the idea that there is somewhere to go and something to get.

This question What is true? is always pointing at something new because what is true in any moment is always changing. So, when you see the truth that this question points you to, the movement of life doesn't end; all that ends is the idea that it is your job to make life turn out a certain way—in a way that is "good for you." That idea is the source of suffering, and that is what gets dissolved by this question.

This question, like any good compass, is only useful when you go to where it points. It always points *here*, so you follow it *here*—to what's true right now. When you end up *here*, it may not always be glamorous or spiritual, but you won't suffer because you won't be trying to be somewhere else that you think is better.

The extent to which you are still looking out for "me" when you ask this question is the extent that you will suffer. To whatever extent the question What's in it for me? is still in play, you will suffer. If you are trying to get some goodies along the way for "me," then you have wandered off of the truth of *what is* right now. The suffering is equal to the distance between here-and-now and what you have given your heart to. If you have given your heart to here-and-now, you won't suffer; but if you have given it to how it could be or should be or how it was or will be, then you have drifted from the truth and you will suffer.

The end of suffering is here and now, and it is immediately available. All you have to do is give up the story—the idea "me"— and the distance disappears, leaving only *what is*. You surrender to whatever is present in this moment, including your own suffering. When you do that, you can't call it suffering anymore because you're no longer taking it personally; the suffering is just part of *what is*. Just realizing the foolishness of wanting things to be different frees you from that desire and the suffering that goes with it. You can let your story and your desires be what they are; you don't have to change them. Illusions are not a problem when they are seen to be illusions.

What about pain, like I'm feeling in my tooth right now?

What is present right now in your mouth?

Sensation.

Yes. What is sensation? Bring your curiosity to it. It's amazing how exquisitely alive a nerve ending can be and how much of our consciousness it can take up. A whole world can be going on around us, and one nerve ending is getting all of our attention. Nerve endings are amazing structures. What is it like to have these sensations in your mouth?

It's frustrating.

This is telling a story about the pain. Could you just let it be that way?

That's what is happening now. So, pain is just sensation?

Someone once said that pain is sensation plus fear, or resistance to the sensation. You can't have pain unless you have both of those. Pain is sensation plus the story you tell yourself about it. You can't change what story is present, but you can see that it is a story. The untrue compass is always trying to resolve the story by getting rid of the sensation. The other compass—what's true right now—points at the sensation, and you are just present to how amazing sensation by itself is.

We are often afraid that if we do this, we'll be so fascinated with sensation that, for instance, we won't take our hand off of a hot stove. But the sensation is very wise, and there is a reason for it. If you stay with the sensation, you can discover what is true about it. Sometimes what is true is that it is only sensation and there is nothing you have to do about it, and other times what is true is that you need to see a dentist. The story only gets in the way of this wisdom. It is a detour on the way to what is real. What is it like right now to have pure sensation?

I'm not aware of it now.

Often, when the story is gone, the sensation turns out to be something different than what you thought it was or the sensation, itself, changes. Like everything else, sensation comes and goes.

The Movement of Awareness

One of the observable qualities of this mystery called Awareness, or Consciousness, is that it comes with a zoom function, like a video camera. It is possible to focus Awareness very narrowly on a particular sensation, emotion, or thought and then to pull the zoom in the other direction, to back up and expand the scope of awareness. There is actually no limit to how far Awareness can go; it can expand to include vast, limitless space, until the known universe is just a speck of dust. This flexibility is just one capacity, or quality, of Awareness.

Another capacity of Consciousness is to become fixed. We have all kinds of words for that: desire, identification, grasping. We become fixated on a particular emotion or identified with a particular desire or try to hold on to a particular experience. This capacity to fixate applies to all levels of consciousness, to both contracted and expanded states. We all know how easy it is to become fixated in contracted states. We sometimes identify so closely with a contracted state like sadness that we even say "I am sad," rather than recognizing that sadness is not something we are but just something we feel in that moment. When the zoom is in the backing up position and we're experiencing beautiful, cosmic realms, we can get fixated there as well, which can result in the formation of a "spiritual ego." We all have seen plenty of examples of this tendency to build an identity around that expanded view, of people who have identified so fully with the Absolute that they think they are beyond the concerns of daily life and beyond having to be accountable for their actions.

Trying to hang on to something is the definition of suffering, whether you are hanging onto pain or onto bliss. You can suffer just as much over the loss of your bliss as the loss of $100,000 in the stock market. The good news is that there is an opposite movement of consciousness, which is the movement of surrender, of release, of love. The *really* good news is that surrender— allowing things to be as they are—is possible at any time. You don't have to wait for a spiritual experience or an expanded state in order to love, to let go, to surrender and to be done with suffering. Love is not dependent on any state.

The invitation is not to wait for a particular state to arise but to just go ahead and love. You can do it right now. You can turn toward everything that is present right now and say yes to it. Let go of any need to have the zoom lens be in one place or another, to have your experience take one form or another. Just love it the way it is.

Sometimes I get overwhelmed by anxiety.

Have you ever seen what a skin mite looks like through an electron microscope? It looks like something from a science fiction movie. Anxiety is caused by a narrowing of attention, like putting something under an electron microscope. When you narrow your attention down, what you narrow it down on seems big—all that is left is that bug. This is one of the capacities of Awareness. It's not you doing it but the Mystery itself. It has the capacity to experience something very small as very big. In fact, in can seem so big that it blocks out everything else. If you blew up a picture of a skin mite to two stories high, it would block out a lot of the rest of the world.

Whenever you blow an idea up, it seems like you have lost the Mystery. This is where you have to ask yourself, Is it true? Is what you are calling a problem really so big? When you go back to the real world, where skin mites are crawling around on your eyebrows, that isn't a problem, is it? Now, the skin mite doesn't even register on the senses.

What happens if you take the zoom so far back that it gets stuck in that mode and keeps going? How big a problem are skin mites then? How big a problem are empty bank accounts or anything else that might generate anxiety? From that place, how big a problem is it to get a job to take care of the empty bank account? That's not a problem either. This isn't about abandoning the body and life. Even Ramana, who zoomed so far out that he let insects and rats gnaw on his legs, eventually re-engaged in this world. Once you have experienced fully zooming out, then zooming in is also no problem.

There isn't anything better or truer about the zoomed-out perspective, the perspective of the Absolute, of Oneness. It's wonderful when we first discover that we can zoom out, but if you think that is everything, then you are not seeing the whole truth, which is that Awareness also zooms in.

Eventually, you realize that if there is no "you," then it doesn't matter whether you are zoomed in or zoomed out. You lose interest in the zoom control, in trying to make Consciousness be different than what it is. If Consciousness zooms way out, fine— so what if bugs chew on your legs? If it zooms way in, fine—it's kind of fun looking into a microscope. At that point, you take your hands off the zoom control and relax.

Conscious Self-Consciousness

Have you ever had a kink in your neck and found yourself testing it all day long to see if it was still there? Self-consciousness is like that. It is the act of constantly referring back to the idea "me." Am "I" still here? How am "I" doing? How is it going for "me"? It's that checking, evaluating, and reflecting on the self that occurs throughout our day. The reason self-consciousness causes suffering is that it refers back to something that doesn't exist. It's checking for how "I" am doing when there is no such thing as "I." Furthermore, this checking usually results in some judgment about "I." Even if the judgment is a positive one, you still suffer because of the concern over how to keep it that way.

Consciousness without this self-consciousness is very ordinary, very present, very alive, and free of suffering. We've all had many experiences of pure Consciousness, when self-consciousness falls away and we are present. They often come when we are struck with beauty or awe or when we are brought into the moment for some other reason. Athletes talk about these moments as "playing in the zone" or "playing out of their minds." These are moments when they are just playing and not reflecting on themselves. All of Consciousness is focused on what is happening, on the next movement of the game. These are often the moments when an athlete does something remarkable.

Sometimes these moments happen in an emergency, when there's no time to check or evaluate how "you" are doing or how this will look on a resume. There is only time to be present. Some people even become attracted to dangerous situations because this experience of no self-consciousness is so alive. What really happens in these moments is that you just forget to check and self-reflect. This natural aliveness can spring forth in very ordinary moments too, like when you are engrossed in a book or just very involved in life. We have all had moments such as these.

So now, the obvious question is: How do you get from self-consciousness to no self-consciousness? The dilemma is that anything "you" do to move yourself from self-consciousness to no self-consciousness is by its nature a form of self-consciousness. In trying to move yourself into no self-consciousness, you have to step into self-consciousness. Anything you try to do just piles on another layer of self-consciousness. For example, after hearing this, you are likely to go home and try not to be self-conscious. You can see how asking yourself, "Am I being self-conscious?" just sets you up for more suffering. This is the dilemma of our effort to be free of the suffering caused by self-consciousness.

Fortunately, there is a way out of this dilemma—a loophole, a backdoor to unselfconsciousness. The loophole is that Consciousness is what is doing this self-consciousness and self-reflection. So, rather than having to unravel the self-consciousness to get to pure Consciousness, you just have to see that pure Consciousness is already right here in this moment of self-consciousness. Even when we are most painfully involved in self-consciousness, pure Consciousness is absolutely and completely present. Simply asking, Who is self-conscious? immediately brings you to this recognition. Once this is seen, there is naturally less and less interest in "me" and more and more interest in everything else. This frees Consciousness up from the futile task of trying to figure out how "I" am doing and allows it to be present to everything else that is happening.

Grace is the fact that Consciousness is always here. Consciousness is like the most unbelievably loyal friend: you could rob him, beat him, sleep with his spouse, kidnap his children; and when you finally turn to him with an open heart, he forgives it all and says, "Oh yes, of course, that was just what you had to go through. I understand." Grace and Consciousness are the same thing. The reason I use the word "grace" is because Consciousness has so much graciousness that even after making ourselves and others terribly miserable for years with our self-consciousness, as soon as we turn and look, this mystery called Consciousness is there completely, without conditions.

Animals are beautiful examples of unselfconsciousness. And yet, there is an added richness in being human because animals haven't gone into the experience of self-consciousness and *then* seen that there is Consciousness even in that; animals are just naturally unselfconscious, so they naturally move with grace and live their lives out of that spontaneous expression of Consciousness. Self-consciousness is not a mistake. It's an opportunity to find out that pure Consciousness can even play the game of self-consciousness and not be trapped in it.

This place of no self-consciousness is a very ordinary experience and it's available right now, even in your moments of self-consciousness. The end of suffering is not at all dependent on becoming good at being unselfconscious. All it depends on is being willing to look and see what is true even about self-consciousness— that even when self-consciousness is present, pure Consciousness is present as well and is in fact the architect of the game. Pure Consciousness is playing all the parts of the game.

PART 6

Approaching the Mystery

the mystery
of this simple moment
cannot be spoken
yet all of history
occurred to arrive here

  the mystery
  of the endless terrain of self
  cannot be mapped out
  countless new frontiers
  are born with every breath
  the mystery
  of awakening
  cannot be achieved
  all that is needed
  is to notice inner eyes that never close
  the mystery
  of sweet undying love
  cannot be understood
  the heart already knows
  what the mind can only long for

the mysteries
always remain
untouched by worried thought
ready to welcome us home
when we abandon our dreams

Living Without a Formula

One of the mind's favorite games is trying to find formulas. The idea is that if you have enough of the right formulas, you won't have any more problems. The mind applies formulas to simple things, like how to make a fluffy omelet and how to change a flat tire, and even to more complicated and unpredictable things, like how to have a good marriage, how to be successful, all the way up to how to become free of suffering. The mind doesn't know when to stop. It tries to apply formulas to everything, even to things that formulas will never work for. Life is too mysterious, too full of surprises, too alive to ever fit a formula, but the mind keeps trying nevertheless.

When you approach life with a formula, you end up with an idea of how things should be, which rarely matches how things actually turn out. For example, one formula might be: if I'm nice to people, they'll be nice to me. This sounds good, but we all know it doesn't always work that way. The problem with formulas is that when our expectations aren't met, we suffer. Suffering comes from this gap between how we think things should work and how they actually are working in the moment. For a long time, what we do in the face of this is try to improve our formulas, with the ultimate goal of creating a "me" that has all the answers, which is an impossible and exhausting project.

The alternative is to let go of all formulas. If you don't have any idea of how things are supposed to be, then there is no suffering, no tension—no sense of things not being right. What you are left with is this messy, beautiful thing called life, unfolding as it always has.

There is no way around this tendency of the mind. This is why many spiritual teachings are packaged as formulas even though they aren't meant to be. One of these is Ramana's practice of self-inquiry: asking, Who am I? It sounds like a formula and yet it was never Ramana's intention that an answer be found. He knew that any belief or concept that showed up as an answer to that question would be exposed as faulty. If that question is asked sincerely, it has the power to dissolve your concepts, beliefs, and formulas. It burns away whatever is in the way of your natural happiness.

There are actually two questions at the center of spiritual life for which there are no formulas: Who am I? and How do I live my life? This is a beautiful pair of questions, which point in two different directions. Who am I? points to the Absolute, while How do I live my life? brings you back down to the challenges of day-to-day existence. If taken together, these questions point us to both the absolute truth of our being and to the relative truth of day-to-day life. When we take both of them together, a dance between the absolute mystery of our being and day-to-day life can happen.

Most of us really like the question How do I live my life? Our minds like to get involved with that one because it seems like it might have a formula. That's why I am also pointing to this other question Who am I? which takes us beyond the mind. That is the question that needs to be asked first, and the *how* will then take care of itself. My teacher, Neelam, in response to most questions would say: "First things first. Find out who you are, and then see if this problem still makes any sense." So, I invite you to put all of your effort every moment into this question Who am I? When you are busy taking care of life, ask: Who is doing this? Who is it that is cooking? Who is it that is driving? Then, your energy goes into this rather than the *how*, while the *how* is just being allowed to happen. This is the opposite of how most of us have been trained to live our lives. We're taught to keep as busy as possible and not look into this question Who am I?

If Who am I? is asked honestly, the only answer you find is a fantasy, a lie. The idea "I" has no actual correspondence to the bigger mystery of who you are. The question Who am I? brings you back to the present moment, which doesn't fit into any of your formulas or ideas about how it should be. Have you ever noticed how the present moment never matches up to how you think it should be? It never quite makes it. Who am I? is the question that pulls the plug on all of your lies and misconceptions. We find very creative ways of avoiding this question because then we can avoid the here and now and keep hiding out in how we would like it to be or how we think it should be. In particular, we hide out in the false idea we call "I," which is the source of all our problems. That's why the effort should go into finding out who you are if you want your suffering to end: "First things first."

If you ask either of these questions sincerely, they take you to the same place: here and now. This day-to-day existence *is* the Mystery—it's not separate from it—and there is no formula for it. The good news is that when you stay in the here and now, you discover you don't need a formula. Life knows how to live. It has never had a formula, and it has done a perfectly good job up to now, but you only discover that when you stay right *here*.

Curiosity and Resting

One of the great gifts of Ramana's teachings is their utter simplicity. He taught that there are two paths to self-realization. One is inquiry, which I often refer to as "curiosity"—being curious about what is true. The other path he mentions is that of surrender. I often use the word "resting" for that—letting everything be the way it is. How utterly simple, to let everything be the way it is!

You can do it with both hands tied behind your back; and yet, we find so many ways to distract ourselves from resting in *what is*.

This is the central dilemma of spiritual life: what we really want is the Truth, and yet we are distracted endlessly by other things. To the extent that you surrender to and inquire about this mystery called life, there is an end to your suffering; and to the extent that you pursue anything else, you suffer. So, why do we struggle so when our truest desire is so readily available?

The simple reason is that there is a payoff in pursuing the desires, the addictions, and the distractions. The payoff is that you get to feel like someone special; you get to pretend that your life is important in an inflated sense. What must be surrendered is that specialness, that sense of being more important than you really are. These distractions pump up the idea of being someone, while surrendering and inquiring is a subtraction process—a process of subtracting all of the illusions about yourself.

It's important to recognize the payoff because then you can decide if it is worth it. Has anything you have done to pump up your sense of self ever been enough? Has it ever satisfied? If you are honest, you have to say no. It has only increased your separation, and separation is painful. Rather than satisfying, it has only increased your longing for something truer, because the farther you go into distractions and away from what is true, the greater the illusion of separation.

Fortunately, no matter how wrapped up you have become in some distraction, when you surrender, you are instantly home. Something instantly opens when you get curious about what is really going on. It's not gradual; there is no in-between: either you are surrendered and no longer suffering or you're not, and your suffering remains.

The good news is that surrender is instantly and always available; the bad news is that anything other than surrender is bound to cause suffering. That's not to say that there aren't pleasant moments; this world wouldn't be a well-designed addiction if it didn't have moments of joy. The only way it could lure you into this illusion of separation is by giving you little tastes of sweetness along the way.

This fundamental truth that freedom is instantly and always available is true before, during, and after what we call awakening. In spiritual circles, there is a lot of emphasis on awakenings—and rightly so; there is nothing like a direct experience of Truth to make these truths real. However, even after a profound awakening, in the very next breath, you are, again, left with the choice of surrendering to the truth of the moment or not.

* * *

The real job of any teacher is to make themselves irrelevant. Once the spirit of curiosity has been fully awakened, you are free from the need for any teacher because your willingness to question takes you to the *source* of Truth. Then, there is no difference between a teacher and a student; neither has more Truth than the other. After awakening, your teachers are no longer the exclusive source of the truth.

Curiosity is the willingness to look and ask questions: Who am I? What is always present? What is feeling pain? What is feeling bliss? What is curious? Where does curiosity come from? After asking such questions, the next step is to rest in what you have discovered. Once you have asked the question, the Truth reveals itself, and you just rest in the truth of your being. You surrender to what is seen. Resting is just another word for surrendering to the truth of who you are.

Without also resting, questioning by itself can actually become a way of keeping the Truth at arms length after it is seen by rushing to ask more questions rather than surrendering to what is being seen in that moment. Questioning has both the power to take you to the Truth and the power to take you right past it by keeping you from looking at it for very long.

Neelam tells a story about a lifelong seeker who had looked everywhere for Truth. Then, one blessed day, he comes across the house of God. He rushes up the stairs, reaches for the doorknob, and suddenly stops, as he realizes that if he opens the door, the story of his life will end: there will be nothing left for him to seek. He will lose his identity as a seeker. So, he pulls back his hand, slips off his shoes so that no one inside the house will hear him leave, and starts back down the path. Now his spiritual seeking has been greatly simplified—he knows he can go anywhere except to that house. Resting is being willing to open the door and surrender to what has been discovered.

* * *

Resting is a recognition of the Absolute Truth, this spacious perfection we're all dancing in, which is, in fact, who we are. In this culture, which is so action-oriented, we need permission to rest; we need to hear that freedom and perfection are already here and that we don't have to do anything to achieve them. What a revelation it is to discover this! We never think of looking in stillness, in the here-and-now, to find the Truth; we are always so busy looking outside ourselves with the mind.

Once the Absolute is seen through resting, a subtle grasping to hold on to that often arises, which is only natural. Who wouldn't want to hang out where everything is seen in its utter perfection? Discovering this perfection is such a relief. However, whenever we fixate anywhere, even in the Absolute, the life drains out of life, like living in a memory. This is why it is not uncommon for people to have an awakening and then feel disillusioned six months later. The Truth hasn't stayed fresh and alive.

This is where curiosity, the other half of resting, comes in. Curiosity keeps whatever quality of the Mystery you are experiencing from getting stale. If you are experiencing peace, for instance, asking, Who or what is experiencing peace? or Where does this peace come from? will keep it fresh and alive. Without this curiosity, the mind will take even something like peace and say, "Oh yeah, more peace—how boring."

Curiosity keeps you from landing in the Absolute and hiding there. It keeps you paying attention—noticing—what is true now in *this* moment. Papaji used the word "vigilance" for this, although no word really captures it. What is called for is both vigilance and curiosity but also, somewhat paradoxically, surrender. When, by grace, the Truth is revealed, the question always is, Will you surrender to it? You have to be willing to give your whole life to the Truth, not just admire it or hide in it. Surrendering to it means being willing to step into and take on the perspective of Emptiness, where there is no such thing as "me" or any thing else apart from it.

Then, what a wonderful surprise it is to discover that from the perspective of Absolute Emptiness *everything* matters. Everything is unutterably precious. The Absolute has an incredible love for the human and for this world, with all its messiness, confusion, and imperfections. It is surprising how much it cares, although it is an impersonal caring. If everything is unspeakably precious, what does that mean? How would that be expressed in the world? It's obviously not through grasping, which no longer makes sense. What would you push away? What would you try to hang on to? Everything is equally precious.

The spiritual life is not about getting to the Absolute. It's not a one-way ticket out of town, away from your problems and the messiness of this world. It's a round-trip ticket: you get to come back and live this life *as* the Absolute. What could that mean? This is where curiosity comes in because the answer to that can only be revealed in each new moment.

Honesty

Many of you have had a taste of the power of the honesty of admitting your pain, confusion, anger, and limitations. Being honest about these things takes you beyond pretending, denying, or resisting those things, which is a big relief. The alternative, which is keeping these hidden and putting up a front, is so much effort and trouble and never works in the end. However, to be completely honest, you also must be willing to admit to the love, the joy, and the Truth that *is* seen. People often say, "I know limitless love is always present, but . . ." and then they describe some struggle they are having. The funny thing about "but" is that it negates everything that came before it. A simple way to be more honest is to replace "but" with "and." Then, there is no negating going on: "Yes, love is present *and* . . . ." When you include everything that is true, you are being completely honest.

Being completely honest will quickly take you beyond what you know to the Truth that is not knowable. If you look at something you say, such as "I am tired," with the intention of being honest, you realize that being tired is not the whole truth. Tiredness is just something that is appearing; it's not who you are. When your intention is for the truth, you quickly arrive at a place of not knowing: you don't know who you are; you don't even know what tiredness is. Who you are is a profound mystery and so is tiredness. All it takes to see this is honesty.

One of the questions you can ask when something is troubling you is, Is it true? If this question is asked sincerely, it is like a fire that burns everything. False concepts can't get past it. All of our concepts are false because they always leave out part of the truth. You can see how, when you are completely honest, you quickly get to the place where you leave concepts behind and everything is a mystery. That is a place that, in spite of its nakedness, is very alive, very real. To whatever degree you are being honest, life is enlivened.

Beyond speaking the truth is living the truth. You not only admit what is true but you surrender your words and actions to it. You live only what you know, even when this means often living in a place of not knowing. You live life as if it is a mystery, not as if you already know everything. That is a more complete kind of honesty.

You don't have to wait for a profound spiritual awakening to live your honesty. Something I often hear is "I know all this, but I still don't experience Freedom." Before, during, and after the experience of Freedom is the even greater possibility of living your honesty. Even if you only have a sliver of the truth, even if you only have a vague sense that love is present, what matters is how much you live from that, how much you act and speak and rest in the truth that you do know.

Don't wait for a spiritual experience to surrender to the Truth. If one comes, that is beautiful; but in the meantime—right now— what do you really know? What is true? Are you willing to give your heart to that? Are you willing to surrender to the love that is already here instead of waiting for a new, improved version to show up?

The Dance Between the Ordinary and the Extraordinary

Today, I'm going to point toward ordinariness. Much of our striving and effort is an attempt to make life extraordinary—to make it better, to get more of this or that. However, the problem with an extraordinary experience, such as expanded consciousness, is that one of two things happens: either it goes away and you are back to the ordinary or you find a way to stay in it and then it becomes ordinary. Whether your extra-ordinary experience sticks around or disappears, you end up back in very ordinary experience.

A funny thing happens when, instead, you become very present to ordinary experience: it becomes extraordinary. When you are present to an ordinary experience, it reveals its extraordinary-ness; and when an extraordinary experience appears, it soon becomes ordinary. There is an apparent movement back and forth between ordinary and extraordinary.

Once you see that extraordinary experience is actually ordinary and ordinary experience is actually extraordinary, you lose interest in this movement between extraordinary and ordinary, or we could just as easily say between good and bad, comfortable and uncomfortable, interesting and boring. The nature of all these dualities is that they keep dissolving back into each other.

What's left, then, is to get interested in what all of this is happening in. What is it that is experiencing the extraordinary and the ordinary, the good and the bad, the interesting and the boring? Since the particular content of any experience is not worth giving attention to because it is already changing into something else, why get excited about the extraordinary or frustrated with the ordinary? What becomes important is what these experiences are appearing in.

With maturity, we begin to see that everything is both ordinary and extraordinary. The mind doesn't like this because its job is to tell us whether something is ordinary or extraordinary. The mind likes to have this duality going so that it has something to do. To the mind, anything is better than this place where everything is both ordinary and extraordinary and it has nothing to do. When even the Absolute becomes ordinary, what is left for the mind to do?

The dance between the ordinary and the extraordinary doesn't stop just because you stop being interested in it. The dance continues, but there is no longer any resistance to it and, consequently, no longer any suffering. Once we give up trying to make our experience be different than what it is, we are done with suffering. Once we recognize the Mystery within which both the ordinary and extraordinary are occurring, we can let both experiences come and go without being fooled by either of them.

Doing and Non-doing

What do I do with this new recognition?

Most people who ask this are trying to figure out how to fit this vast Mystery into their personal life and their old idea of who they are—and it's the other way around. The question is, How will you serve the Mystery? The only way you can answer this is to look in the Mystery and find out what is true right now. We can't know now what will be true for tomorrow or a year from now; we can only know what is true right now. Right now, what is the Mystery calling you to do?

* * *

I've heard that to awaken you have to let go of wanting to awaken. I have trouble with this because I want to awaken more than anything else.

Has anything you have tried worked so far? In the end, that desire also gets left behind because the idea that there is something called "enlightenment" or "awakening" and the idea that there is someone who awakens are seen as faulty. In the meantime, if the desire to awaken is present, you can't decide to not want it. If wanting it is present, then wanting it is present. Again, I invite you to look closely at the question I just asked you, Has anything ever worked? Is there anything that you can do?

I've also heard that the yearning will take you there, and that really confuses me if you also have to let go of the yearning to get there.

The yearning and the truth that you can't do anything about it are like two grinding stones, which grind up all the other desires, illusions, and distractions. I just want to reassure you that everything that gets ground up never existed anyway. It never amounted to anything, so it's like throwing away your useless junk. So, yes, both are true: you want it and there is nothing you can do about it. What happens right now when you allow both of those to be present? What is that like?

It makes me feel like crying.

When you just allow that, what is even deeper than the sadness that wells up?

Feeling totally lost.

That's the mind coming up against that which it can't contain. And when you allow that (it takes a lot of allowing), what is beneath even that? What is present right now?

What am I going to do?

That's going back into the mind. What is beneath all that? First, you have to allow the fact that you're really lost, which is how it has always been; but then sink a little deeper. What is the Heart's experience right now?

Nothing.

This is the Truth. Just look into that nothing and don't stop when you come up against the absolute emptiness of the mind. What is present right now in this nothing? What is already here?

You're sly.

There is something in this nothing isn't there? It's the last place you would have thought to look for it, isn't it? The mind still has no idea what it is, right? If you bring the mind back, it would still be totally confused.

My mind keeps asking, "What am I going to do with this body?"

Does this Mystery that is present even in nothing have any problem with this body? We habitually return to the mind and emotions to see how things are going. That's a problem regardless of what is present because if a good emotion is present, you struggle to keep it, and if a bad emotion is present, you struggle to get rid of it. So, if you keep checking there, you will never be done struggling and suffering.

When you check, is the Mystery lacking anything? You have to go to the Mystery to answer that, not the mind. When you just stop and check, the Emptiness is still present even when the mind comes in, isn't it? Is there anything lacking in this Mystery?

The fact that it won't last.

But it's here, right now, isn't it? Just check in the Mystery, not in the mind, and tell me if it has ever not been here. Can you find a place or a time outside of this Mystery?

When I go to the Mystery, I get back to this nothing.

Go even beyond that. The mind interprets this nothingness, this emptiness, as a mistake and a reason to look elsewhere. I'm inviting you to notice what is present even in nothing. Even in the midst of this nothingness, there is something aware of the nothingness, or you wouldn't be able to tell me about it, would you?

And you're sure that that is not the mind?

Just check. What is aware of the mind?

It's a presence.

When you check in that, can you find a time or place when it has not been present? The purpose of asking you these questions is not to get an answer from you but to keep pointing you back to the Mystery. Awareness, itself, is a mystery. What is it? Just keep looking even when you come up against nothingness or when the mind gets scared or confused.

When I go back into the Awareness, nobody is aware—it's not me! Who is aware? I can't even say it is "I."

This is being honest. When you actually look, you can't find something called "I"; you just find more Awareness, more Mystery. The illusion that there is such a thing as "I" dissolves under such scrutiny.

What about the suffering in the world? Does the idea that everything is just the way it should be imply complacency? I don't think so.

The idea that everything is perfect and therefore nothing matters can be used as an excuse to indulge oneself, or worse, for horrible abuses of power. The only valuable starting place is the *whole* truth. Part of the truth is that no harm is done, even by the most horrible acts or events, because this Mystery that we all are is not damaged by anything. If you leave that part of the truth out and see only the horror, then your actions will come from only half of the truth, which usually results in imposing more violence upon the violence.

The other part of the truth is that *everything* matters. If you only take into account the part of the truth that everything is perfect and therefore nothing matters and leave out the part that everything matters, you won't feel a need to do anything about the suffering. This is what is called "hiding out in the Absolute." The goal of spiritual life is not to transcend the world or be done with it but to bring the Absolute *to* the suffering of the world. You do this simply by bringing the perspective of the Absolute into the experience of suffering that is arising here and now. Recognizing the whole truth that both nothing and everything matters makes this possible.

Then, an even deeper question arises: What is the source of suffering? If you look into your own experience, you will see that suffering doesn't come from not getting what you want but from wanting. And, if you look even deeper, wanting comes from believing you are separate from the Whole. You could only feel a lack of something if you felt separate from the Whole because nothing is lacking in the Whole. How could the Whole want anything? It makes no sense to want something you already have. So, suffering comes from believing that you are a separate someone.

For a long time I thought I was the one deciding to do things, but I see that thoughts just appear and doing occurs. Then, the task ends, and there is this empty place until the next thought to do occurs. There's no feeling of effort, just this watching for something to arise.

Yes. There is no *personal* effort. There is actually a lot of effort, though, like what you've been doing with your hands as you've been speaking, but there is no quality of *my* to it. If it is mine-less, there is an ease to it; it just flows. Like you said: a thought pops up and you do it and then forget about it because it's done.

What you described has actually been true of every thought and action that has ever taken place in the whole universe, including the thought that something applies to *me*. You didn't decide to have that thought either. It had its unfoldment. It may be more like a weed than a flower, but weeds have their place. The only choice is to be honest about what is arising since you have no choice about what arises. Once you are honest, the ego doesn't dissolve; it is just exposed as never having existed. It is just a thought. There is no ego to get rid of. Freedom is the recognition that there is no ego—and never has been. You just have to be willing to look at everything that has ever been done and see that it has never been you doing it.

Embracing Feelings

Lately, I've been feeling depressed. How do you embrace the experience of being down?

Embracing, or welcoming, is simply not resisting the feeling. You don't have to do something; you only have to be willing to stop and be where you are. That opens the space for Love. You don't have to make Love happen; all you have to do is tell the truth about what is already here, including the Love. It's a lot of work pretending that something isn't happening. What happens when you let these feelings of depression be present just the way they are? Don't try to get away from them or fix them; just let them be here.

Nothing is happening.

That's the truth. When you do that, nothing happens. This doesn't mean you're doing something wrong. Just stay here in this place of nothing happening, in this place where these feelings are just the way they are. Just notice what happens when you rest here. Is nothing still happening?

Yes.

Good. Those are the correct results.

There's some resistance.

Just let that be here too. Just take a little time off from trying to fix this or be done with it. Then, notice what is also present besides the feelings and resistance. Only when you stop and let all of that be for a moment is there the possibility of noticing what else is present. One thing you can notice is that there is room for all of it. If it's here, there must be room for it. That can be a surprise.

There's so much grief too.

Is there room for the grief? Is it a problem?

No. It feels like love is behind it. It's like a game you've played a long time that you know you have to let go of because it's run its course. It's just a call to come home.

That is all it has ever been. Is this call pulling you into Love right now?

I'm resisting.

There is even room for that. What is Love's perspective on this resistance? Love is here also, so try looking out of its eyes at the resistance. Does Love have any problem with it?

It doesn't care.

It just loves. It's going to love you anyway, even though you are resisting it. You truly can't do anything to make this Love go away. You have tried everything, and it's still here and not the least bit diminished by any of your efforts.

It says, "Resistance is futile!"

No matter how long it takes, the outcome is certain: love will win the war. In your heart, you already know that.

* * *

I'm filled with sadness. There's sadness around me, around my personal life, and sadness over the people who were just bombed a few hours ago. I don't even know these people, but it is affecting me. The only two feelings I have are love and sadness.

Which one is bigger, love or sadness?

The one that is more present is the sadness.

Yes, but you know in an eclipse, the moon can block out the sun; and yet, the sun is much bigger than the moon. To answer this question, you have to go to the core of both of these feelings. Does love come out of sadness or does sadness come out of love?

Sadness arises from the love.

Yes. If you didn't have so much love, you'd have no reason to be sad about the situation. Love is the ground, or source, of all feelings. Does the Love have any problem with the sadness?

No.

This is the difference between checking in your feelings and checking in the Love. If you just check in your feelings, you are likely to get caught up in trying to fix or change the sadness. But if you check in the Love, you'll see that there is room for the sadness. There is room for even more sadness. Right now, if there were ten times as much sadness, would Love, or the Heart, have any problem with that? It's big enough for infinite amounts of sadness, isn't it? Just see what happens when you experience even this much sadness from the perspective of this loving Mystery.

Inquiry and Devotion

Although curiosity and resting may seem like a prescription for what to do, you don't actually *do* them. Rather, they are *descriptions* of what is already and always occurring: Awareness allows things to be as they are, and it is by nature curious and therefore engages with whatever it is aware of. Spiritual practices simply create an alignment that allows you to recognize the depth of resting and curiosity, and other qualities, that are already present in Awareness.

A simple example of this is the practice of meditation, which requires sitting still. If you don't move the body, that stillness resonates with the Silence that everything appears in. Being still allows you to recognize the ever-present Silence, which is another quality of Awareness. It brings the outer into alignment with the inner. There is no need to create stillness; Stillness is the underlying reality.

Spiritual practices, such as Ramana's self-inquiry, fall into two categories, which correspond to curiosity and resting. Self-inquiry— questioning everything—falls under the category of curiosity and is part of the spiritual path called *jnana*, which is a Sanskrit word for knowledge. Inquiring creates an alignment, which drops you into that curiosity that is innate to Awareness. Even Ramana spoke of self-inquiry as something you do only until this alignment has occurred. When you have practiced self-inquiry enough, it eventually resonates to and reveals this innate curiosity.

The other category of spiritual practices is focused on devotion, which relates to resting. The path of devotion, or *bhakta*, is one of continually saying yes to life and tapping into Awareness' innate capacity to love by being present and allowing things to be the way they are. The practices of this path—singing, dancing, poetry, and prayer—create a doorway into the Heart.

The devotional path unravels the ego by continually surrendering to love and by loving more than the ego can withstand, while the path of inquiry accomplishes this by questioning so deeply that our illusions, especially the illusion "me," don't hold up. Since both paths take you to the same place, which path you follow doesn't matter; what does matter is how completely you are engaged in them.

Inquiry is very effective for dealing with negative emotional states and experiences by asking, To whom is this discomfort or unpleasant experience arising? However, many who practice self-inquiry stop inquiring once they reach a positive state because they see no reason to continue. The problem with this is that the effect brought about by the inquiry won't last. So, the suggestion is to practice self-inquiry all the time, whether something good or bad is showing up. Find out what is present in both the good and bad states and experiences. If you are willing to continue the inquiry even when beautiful things like bliss show up, a new sense of freedom arises. It no longer will matter when the bliss goes away, as it inevitably will. When inquiry is total, it crosses the line from being a mental exercise to something that breaks your heart open. It becomes more grounded in devotion, or resting and allowing. At its root, it turns out that curiosity and resting are aspects of the same thing.

Those drawn to a devotional path have the opposite problem. It is easy to love everything when your heart is being burst open by devotional practices and you are flooded with bliss; what is difficult is practicing devotion when life becomes unpleasant. Just as with self-inquiry, if you are going to use devotion as a prescription, you have to be complete about it. The description of Awareness is that it is already in love and devoted to *everything*. So, when that difficult person, situation, or emotion shows up, you give it the same devotion you would give the Divine. You treat it with overwhelming gratitude. If you are devoted even when the world shows up in unpleasant ways, it takes you to a place where curiosity is elicited about this Mystery.

With this kind of completeness of inquiry or devotion, the boundary between practice and the truth of who you are dissolves; spiritual practice and Truth come together. Completeness is what is crucial. The way these prescriptions become descriptions is by giving yourself totally to them and not just applying them at certain times—by not being too busy feeling good to inquire or too busy feeling bad to give love.

Stepping into the Unknown

Trust is developed in childhood from the type of "holding" we received when we were young. No one received perfect holding— no one was held for the first six years of life and never put down! What that created was the illusion that this Mystery can't be trusted. The problem is that the only way to regain that trust is to step into the Mystery. Trust can't be regained by trying to understand the Mystery intellectually, and nothing I say can take the place of stepping into it. In some traditions, they speak of it as an empty-handed leap into the Void because that is what it feels like. It feels like stepping into the unknown because that is the truth about it— that it is not knowable. It is trustworthy; it's just not knowable. The only way to discover that it is trustworthy is to give it all of your attention and not turn away even when it seems like you are stepping into the Void, into nothing.

Devotion to a Guru

I spent the last 22 years in India at the feet of a master, and that is changing. (tears)

What are these tears?

That's my particular form of grasping.

Just grasp then; grab on as tight as you can. If you fight it, you'll never find out what it's about. Let yourself grab on for dear life because that's what you want to do.

I'm afraid to admit that I know who I am. I think I just identify with this particular form of spiritual life. Now I'm living in the West for the first time, and all I want to do is clean and cook and sew. With an Indian master, there is a lot of adoration, and as a woman it is easy for me to do this and it is also very fulfilling.

What if you take that same adoration and put it into the sewing and into the gardening and into whatever it is you are cleaning? That's all. Don't throw your adoration out just because it won't work anymore to pretend it only applies to the guru. Be willing to waste some good adoration on a flower or a bug or someone in the supermarket. What a profound gift you were given to discover this capacity for love, for adoration, for devotion. The gift is to discover that the love is in you and not dependent on the master. What is this? (more tears)

It implies being more alone. I've been saying to my master that the next thing for me is to be alone, and he agreed. There's nothing cozier than to be in a small community with a master.

If something is required for love to happen, that is not Freedom— even if it's something wonderful like a guru. The Mystery loves you too much to let you have less than total freedom. Your heart won't be satisfied until you experience total freedom. As beautiful as living in a community has been for you, if that has become a place of grasping, the Mystery will show you that love is not limited to that.

Do you think men and women have different paths? I've heard it said that women need someone outside themselves.

If you were a woman, then that would be a problem. There is definitely a woman here; I'm not denying your gender, but that is not who you are. What is true? What is your deepest knowing right now?

A feeling of love, which wants to be expressed in living.

Is there a problem here?

No. I get stuck in identification with being a woman.

This idea of being a woman is very convincing, but it's not the whole story. What is Love's perspective on your being identified with being a woman? We never think to ask that. This question is not only for the big questions but also for more mundane questions and any stickiness that arises. When you go deeper by asking this question, nothing changes—you are still a woman—but woman-ness is viewed from something truer. It is recognized as just one expression of what you truly are.

The answers about how to live the next phase of your life will come fresh in the moment. You have to be willing to not know because that is what allows each fresh, new knowing to be discovered. Take the light of Love and step into the dark with it; step into this place where you don't know. You don't know what it will be like to live alone, but that is where the light wants to go; so be willing to step into that place of not knowing.

PART 7

Two Simple Instructions

the passion for freedom
swallows the source of passion
if twoness could lead to oneness
we would all be faithful lovers
no reason to dream of love
for it is already here in the waking heart
find it now
in the sweet infinity
of this moment's
eternal embrace

The Treasure

I'd like to begin by sharing with you, in my own words, a Sufi teaching story: Once upon a time there was a farmer who was very successful and known for his generosity. He had five sons, and as is not uncommon when someone is born into wealth, all of his sons were lazy. When the father was on his deathbed, he called his sons to him and told them that their inheritance was buried in the fields, but then he died before they could get him to tell them where it was.

After he was buried, they grabbed shovels and began digging the fields systematically so as not to miss even a single square inch. Finally, they got down to the last corner and still there was no treasure. Once they got over their frustration and disappointment, they decided to plant something since the fields were already dug up. It turned out to be a good year, and they had a successful crop and were able to live very comfortably for that year.

The following spring, one of the brothers suggested they might have missed the treasure: perhaps they didn't dig deeply enough. So, they got out their shovels and carefully dug the fields again. When they got to the last bit of dirt, the result was the same— nothing. So, once again, they planted the fields, harvested another crop, and lived comfortably another year. This went on for a few more years until at a certain point they kept digging every spring even though they had given up on the buried inheritance. They had gotten into the rhythm of life of farming, of the life they were born to, and lived very successful lives as farmers.

Spiritual seekers are like the sons in this story: they think that spiritual techniques—everything from meditation to inquiry to loving kindness—will get them to some buried treasure called enlightenment, freedom, liberation. And yet, if they stick with a practice long enough, they discover that the practice, itself, is the true treasure.

The Practice

Spiritual practice can be boiled down to two simple instructions. The first is to notice your experience and be curious about it. This is really all that the practice of spiritual inquiry is about. It just points you to the experience you are having right now. Get curious about it. What's going on right now? Who or what is listening? Who or what is breathing? Who or what is thinking? Curiosity is the willingness to see through everything. It is the natural tendency of our being to uncover more.

Noticing your experience and being curious about it brings a deep joy because this is what your being does naturally. It is what your being *is*, actually. You *are* this fundamental awareness and curiosity, or fascination, with every experience. So, awareness and curiosity aren't really something you *do*, but before you realize this, you are given this instruction as a spiritual practice. All this practice does is allow you to recognize your being, which is already noticing and curious about everything.

The second simple instruction is to know that whatever you are experiencing is the right experience and therefore to allow it—to surrender to it. This is what I've been calling resting. Even if you are deep, deep into suffering, that is the right experience. Whatever is happening is what is needed in this moment. You allow things to be the way they are not because it will get you to some buried treasure but because it is the only honest thing to do: things are the way they are. When you do this, you find that there is something very satisfying about the truth of every moment, whether it is a moment of struggle or ease.

Allowing things to be the way they are also brings joy for the same reason that noticing and being curious do: it is fundamental to our nature. Allowing isn't really something we do but who we *are*. I like to point out that you are already allowing 99.99% of your experience. For instance, you probably have no problem with most of the sounds in this room or with the ceiling. And what about outside this room? Do you have any problem right now with the stars? If everything outside the solar system is okey-dokey, right there, that takes care of most of the universe.

Regardless of what is happening—whether you are experiencing fear, desire, or cosmic bliss—you can carry out these two simple instructions. However, you can't carry out one of these instructions without carrying out the other: you can't really get curious about something if you are trying to get rid of it, and you can't really allow your experience if you are not present to it. So, there is really only one instruction: notice your experience and know that it is the right experience.

Noticing

You are always noticing your experience. Just try to not to. See if you are able to not notice anything about your experience. You are always noticing things like the temperature of the room, your body's sensations, and what thought or feeling is currently arising. What I'm suggesting is that you include even more of your experience in your awareness.

We usually only pay attention to part of what is going on. We tend to narrow our attention onto the *content* of our experience— onto the particular thoughts, feelings, and desires that are arising— and even more particularly, onto the *content* of these thoughts, feelings, and desires. We become engrossed in the story attached to them. For example, if an emotion is arising, our attention is usually on what evoked it, our conditioning around it, and how to either get rid of or maintain it rather than on the actual experience of it. And if we are having a thought, we usually don't experience thinking as much as we experience the content of that thought. This tendency is especially strong with desires. We build an elaborate fantasy about how to manifest that desire and what it would be like to get it rather than on the experience of desire in that moment. We become so mesmerized by our fantasy that we go to sleep to our actual experience in the moment.

The invitation is to notice not only the content of a thought, feeling, or desire but the *context* in which it is arising. Notice the actual experience of desire or the experience of doing or thinking or feeling, not just the storyline that they have generated. The experiences of thinking, feeling, and desiring are very mysterious. Notice the space in which thinking, feeling, and desiring are happening. Who or what is noticing? The noticer is part of your experience too. Who or what is thinking, feeling, or doing? This is a complete mystery. Where do thoughts, feelings, and actions come from?

When you include the *whole* of your experience, not just the content of it, you discover the deep joy in simply uncovering the truth in this moment, whether this moment is a painful one, a profound one, or an ordinary one. The true joy is in meeting all of life.

This has made me think about how I show up in the moment. What I do is notice my thoughts about what's happening and the pictures in my head, and I try to notice what body sensations are happening too, like where there is tension.

Also notice the actions of your body, simple things like the restlessness being expressed by your foot tapping. Then, also notice your fundamental stance toward the experience. Notice what the noticing is for. Is it just a new, improved way of trying to get away from any discomfort or get more pleasure? Is it just more ammunition for battling with what is or is it true curiosity?

When you do this, you're likely to discover that most of the time your basic stance towards what is happening is one of trying to avoid pain or get pleasure. This is often the underlying unconscious motivation. If that is the case, then just get curious about that. We think that noticing is another technique that will finally fix things. So, we use inquiry this way and then wonder why we continue to suffer. The way you keep inquiry innocent is to include as much of your experience in that moment as you can, and that means not leaving out why you are doing inquiry.

* * *

Where do I put my attention?

You've got plenty—just waste it! Spread it around. Throw it at everything. You've never run out yet, have you?

That's the problem. My attention is everywhere.

Just put your attention on that also. You've got plenty of this Awareness, or Love. What happens if you don't hold it back from anything? It doesn't matter whether what is showing up is a profound thought or an ordinary one, a spiritual thought or an unspiritual thought. What happens when you just keep throwing this attention—this Love—at everything that shows up?

I'm aware of how I've been working at putting my attention only on the right things.

That's where the struggle lies—in trying to have the *right* thoughts. What if you just give this love to all of your thoughts? What happens if you become a slut for experience?

I've been trying to drop out of experience.

How's it going? Everywhere you drop, there's another experience! You don't have to change anything; just get curious about this thing you call dropping out of experience. It doesn't matter if you succeed or fail at it. If you are curious and in love with whatever is showing up, it won't matter to you whether it is a good thought or a bad thought, a good feeling or a bad feeling, a good experience or a bad experience. And if you are curious about a desire that is showing up, it won't matter if it gets satisfied or not.

* * *

Does that curiosity just arise for you? Do you cultivate it? I had an experience the other night while having a headache in which I felt held by the Beloved, and I had no trouble being curious about that. But ordinarily I don't give the truth my full attention. I'm caught up in all my old habits.

Just for a moment, peel away the boundary between the Beloved and all of your ordinary experiences. Is there really a boundary between them? There is deep joy in being curious about the Beloved. What needs to be seen is that it is all your Beloved, even the habits, even the lies. The Beloved went to a lot of trouble to create those lies just so it could give you the joy of seeing through them. You don't have to go looking for the Beloved somewhere else. It's diving into your arms all the time.

The moment you allow your old habits, they aren't your old habits anymore. Besides, there is no such thing as an old habit because you have never had the same experience twice. The one thing this Mystery is incapable of is repeating itself. So, when a so-called habit arises, it is a completely unique experience.

* * *

How do you get curious about being bogged down?

Just let yourself be bogged down. What is it like if you just let it be this way? What is that experience? What is the experience that you are calling "bogged down"?

Being hit in the face with patterns.

Drop into the experience of being caught in a pattern.

What I want to do is talk about the story behind the pattern: this happened when I was ten . . .

If that is what's happening, then that is what's happening. If those thoughts are coming, then those thoughts are coming. It's okay. All I'm saying is to get curious about what this is like, especially if you stop fighting it and just let those thoughts come. What's that like?

It's definitely more comfortable. Ahhhh!

Now that it's more comfortable, does it really matter if these thoughts keep coming? If the joy is in uncovering this moment, then it doesn't have to look any other way than it does.

Maybe the experience of the moment is one of repetitive thought. If you actually experience repetitive thought it can be ecstatic. What a profound mystery! What a wondrous thing! Besides, you never really have the same thought twice. That's the big lie of these so-called patterns. If you are really curious about your experience of each thought, you'll realize that every thought is a completely new experience. This thing we call thought is a profound mystery, and it's showing up in a form right now that it has never shown up in before.

This thing that we are calling "your experience," which I'm telling you to pay attention to and allow, is like a 600-pound wild animal—an unbelievable force of nature. Thought is a completely unpredictable wild animal. And feelings . . . ! And experience—what is that? You can never get hold of it. By the time it registers in your mind, it's already gone.

* * *

Sometimes curiosity has spontaneously come up, and I've been able to surrender to the experience, but that doesn't seem like something I do. It's a kind of grace that just happens. Is there another kind of curiosity that I can do or do I just have to wait for that grace to happen?

Every experience is that grace happening. What is this experience you are calling "no grace"? Is there really such a thing? Can you find a moment in your entire existence when there was no Awareness, no curiosity? Awareness and curiosity are both qualities of your being. We make it sound like a technique, but all I'm doing is describing what has been happening every moment of your existence and telling you to do that. This instruction, to notice your experience and be curious about it, only points you to the seeing and the curiosity that are already happening. Awakeness and curiosity already *are* in every moment. I challenge you to stop being curious. See if you can shut it off.

* * *

What is grace?

Grace is what shows up when you show up, and she's a master of disguise. In one moment, she'll show up as the perfect lover, maybe even literally. In another moment, she'll show up as the worst possible lover, literally or figuratively. Everything that shows up when you show up is grace. Even the painful, mistaken ideas are grace. They are the result of being cut off from something true, so it's a good thing that they are painful because they get our attention so that we can see that they aren't true. The pain is the grace. Every moment is perfect. Every moment is grace. Every experience points to a deeper truth.

Allowing

Noticing requires allowing. To really be aware of your experience as it is, you can't be busy trying to change it. If you're trying to change it, you are not noticing it the way it is. However, we tend to go beyond noticing whatever is happening to trying to fix it or change it. We treat our experience as a project—the "me" project. We are always looking to make whatever is happening more, different, or better than it is. We don't just allow whatever is to just be the way it is. But if whatever is happening is the right experience, that implies allowing it just the way it is.

Once you allow everything to be the way it is, then you can get curious about what is really going on. What is this mystery called awareness or thinking or doing? When you just notice without trying to change anything, it is possible for your awareness to include more of an experience of the *whole* mystery rather than just some of the objects within it.

A funny thing can happen with allowing: we can become complacent. We not only take our hands off the steering wheel but close our eyes and go to sleep to our experience—we disconnect from our experience. We become too passive. One way this manifests is through indulgence. For example, if an emotion like anger is arising, rather than just allowing ourselves to have the experience of anger, we indulge it and express it. We dump our anger on someone or something else. Another way we indulge is by rationalizing: if my experience is always the right experience, then I'll just have another beer or eat some more cookies.

What's missing when this is happening is noticing and really being curious about your experience. Just as noticing requires allowing, allowing requires noticing to stay balanced. You not only allow anger, for example, but you get curious about it before it gets to the point of being expressed or repressed. Both are necessary: noticing your experience as it is and allowing it—not doing anything to change it and not doing anything to move away from it. Both allowing it and being curious about it are necessary. The arising of something like anger or fear or doubt is not a problem, but if you don't become curious about it you will tend to express it.

One way to suffer is to try to fix the moment. Another way is to try to escape the moment. The good news is that in the very next breath, if you become curious about that effort to fix or that attempt to escape, you won't be suffering anymore. You don't have to undo anything or do penance; you only have to be curious about what it is like to try to change the moment or to try to escape from it and then allow the whole of that experience. Whenever you are really present and curious about your experience, you are free. Your suffering is gone.

We all have moments when we neither struggle with the moment nor try to escape it. Often this is when everything is going great. Who wouldn't pay attention then? Who wouldn't allow it then? Whenever there is a meeting of the moment with open eyes and an open heart, the moment opens up and becomes fuller and richer. When you are *there* in the moment, the truth reveals itself. All you have to do is show up in the moment. But when you try to change or get away from the moment, the opposite happens. Your experience gets smaller, tighter, more constricted, and less satisfying.

All that matters is that you meet your experience with everything you've got—an open mind, an open heart, and a surrendered attitude. You surrender to whatever is going on. Eventually you discover that true liberation is in the inquiry, itself, and not in the place that it takes you to. The true joy is the inquiry itself, and that joy comes whether the inquiry is into something profound and wonderful or something not so pretty. The true joy is in seeing the truth. The only thing that really satisfies is uncovering the truth of this moment. What I mean by truth is what is present right here and right now that opens the heart. Until you find that, nothing else will satisfy.

If you meet every experience, nothing can make you suffer. Find out if there is something rich and true in even the most painful moments. Find out what happens if you are intensely curious about your experience just the way it is. Find out what that can unlock and reveal.

It's a lot easier to talk about than to do it.

How hard is it to just meet this experience?

It's probably harder to avoid it.

That's where all the effort is.

It can seem harder.

Get curious about it being hard. Often if it is hard, it means you are not allowing your current experience. Even if it's hard, it is easy to let it be hard. Any moment becomes ridiculously easy when you just allow it to be the way it is.

Have you ever been able to shut off this curiosity? Just like farming was part of the sons' nature, curiosity is part of ours. The only reason for practicing curiosity is to realize your own nature. The farmer's sons finally realized they were farmers. They didn't *become* farmers; they were born farmers. Rather than trying to remember to be curious, just notice that you already are.

* * *

When I dropped my computer and was without it for two weeks, acceptance was difficult. I was really frustrated.

What if, fundamentally, frustration is as rich an experience as getting what you want? Having a broken computer and having a brand new one are very different experiences, but what if both of these events have just as much experience in them? What if the measurement was not how much pleasure or pain is in an experience but how much experience is in an experience?

There's an equal amount.

The only thing that changes is your measuring stick. Pleasure and pain don't go away, but they no longer are your measuring stick. Experience hasn't become free of challenges or problems, but the measurement is no longer whether something is problem-free or not. All that matters is what is happening, which doesn't always match our ideas of what should be happening. You can even get curious about the experience of not accepting if that is what is happening.

* * *

How do you accept boredom?

If you are experiencing boredom, it means that there is something under the surface that hasn't been seen. It's really very simple, just ask: What is true now? Boredom is a place of suffering or you wouldn't call it boredom but peace. So, there must be some resistance present—you want something else to be happening.

If you experience the emptiness at the core of your being only through your mind, you will feel bored and are likely to look for something to fill it up, like TV or eating or shopping. If, instead, you allow a moment where nothing is happening to be empty and you find out what is true about it, you'll discover richness in the most ordinary moments. All of sudden, you might appreciate how the light just shifted when the cloud went behind the sun—nothing exciting. It won't impress your friends or be in the *New York Times* tomorrow, and yet it is a very rich experience.

Just notice and allow whatever is. If boredom arises, pay attention to it and get curious about it. You call it boredom, but do you really know what boredom is? Have you ever really experienced it or have you always grabbed for something to make it go away? And if you are doing that, then just allow that. The only trick to this is to do it with *whatever* is arising in this moment. If resistance to boredom is arising, just allow the resistance and get curious about it.

When you explore your resistance, you are not your resistance because you're exploring it, so it's kind of fun!

There is a deep joy in this exploration of truth.

* * *

So, if I am experiencing pain, then to be harmonious, I need to accept it fully?

Why would you want to be harmonious? Probably to get rid of the pain. The suffering comes from the effort to try to be harmonious or to get rid of the pain.

One should accept pain? Is that the right word?

It's the right word, but you don't accept the pain for any particular reason. You accept it because that is what is happening— because that is what is true in that moment—not because accepting pain will make it go away.

So, as long as there is no ulterior motive . . .

The truth is we're full of ulterior motives. So as long as there are ulterior motives, just accept them also. Get curious about it all.

* * *

Could you explain how, with enlightenment, it is said that you don't have to do anything and yet you have to work hard?

You have to work hard at not doing. You give what is everything you've got and yet you don't do anything to try to change it. You fall in love with what is. Being in love is actually a lot of work, right? To be a good lover, you have to pay attention to the object of your affection. It doesn't feel like work and it's very satisfying, so you do it naturally. Rather than wait for the perfect experience, just fall in love with the whole of your experience the way it already is.

Showing Up

Rather than noticing their experience and knowing that it is the right one, life for most people is about avoiding pain and getting pleasure. Some are more oriented towards pleasure, while others are more oriented towards avoiding pain, but either results in suffering, whether or not they succeed. The effort, itself, to do either of these is the cause of suffering. As long as your focus is on getting pleasure or avoiding pain, you will be miserable. Alternatively, when you just show up in life and have an experience for the sake of having it, whether it is painful or pleasurable, you don't suffer. This is a very simple truth.

We come into every experience empty-handed and we leave every experience empty-handed. Everything you have ever experienced prior to this moment, even the most painful and most pleasurable experience, is irrelevant. And regardless of whether this moment is a painful one or a pleasurable one, in the next moment, that will be irrelevant too. What happens now won't matter an hour from now, and what happened for the last twenty, thirty, forty years doesn't matter now. What matters is showing up for whatever is arising in *this* moment.

When you finally get exhausted by suffering, which is one way that grace works, you find yourself doing things just for the sake of doing them, without any agenda and without any judgment about what is happening or desire to change it. You just notice your experience and let it be the way it is. When you are doing something for its own sake, it doesn't need to be any different than it is. When you are noticing your experience and allowing it just for the sake of noticing and allowing it, then you are free. That is liberation. That is the end of suffering.

Very commonly, we also use this simple truth to try to increase the pleasure in our life or erase the pain. We notice our experience and allow it in order to stop feeling pain or to experience the pleasure from expanded states that often comes from this. Applying these instructions with either of these agendas will cause you to suffer just as much as not applying these instructions. But if you notice and allow whatever is happening just for its own sake, you will be free of suffering—not free of pain, but free of suffering.

This isn't a judgment about seeking pleasure or avoiding pain; this approach to life is just part of the human experience—until it isn't. If that is what's happening, then that is what's happening. The invitation is just to show up for that when that happens— really experience that. Be curious about it. Get really curious about the experience of avoiding pain and the experience of seeking pleasure, and this will bring you very much into the moment.

When you show up in the moment, you often initially encounter all the ways you are trying to get away from the moment. Then, if you show up for this resistance, you see that it is just resistance, and you no longer suffer over it. You don't have to wait to become free of resistance—it still arises—but by embracing it when it arises you become free.

What is it like to be here in this moment without any agenda and without any conclusions, judgments, beliefs, fantasies, or stories between you and the truth of this moment? Being here in the moment requires a willingness to let go of all of your ideas about what is happening and to not know. The more willing you are to look at what is here right now, the less you know; and the less willing you are to see the truth of this moment, the more you rely on what you know.

I sometimes feel apathetic.

The invitation is to show up for every moment. Apathy is a way of not showing up for the moment. That's okay if that is what is happening, then show up for the apathy. We think we shouldn't be feeling apathetic, but there is some jewel of truth in that apathy that needs to be uncovered. The truth that is uncovered may not feel good and it may not be so pretty, but that doesn't matter. In that apathy, is some profound gift, something very real and satisfying. It's the last place we would think to look for satisfaction— in our dissatisfaction.

* * *

If you go to a meeting like this to get something or to feel a certain way and that doesn't happen, you feel like it is a waste of time.

At some point, you start enjoying all the ways you waste your time. You show up for the ways you waste your time. You get the satisfaction *there*, not from some pay-off. You get satisfaction out of just living—just being.

* * *

I feel it takes a lot of energy to maintain awareness, so if I don't feel energetic, then my life isn't the way I want it to be.

The truth is that your life is not going to be the way you want it to be anyway. It's going to be the way it is going to be. It is the way it is. Life doesn't check with you first to find out how you want it to be. Have you noticed that? Sometimes it does turn out the way you want, but your desires don't determine what happens. Find out what doesn't require a lot of energy and maintenance.

* * *

When I get home late from work, I don't go to bed right away because I always have to do something fun or I feel dissatisfied with my day.

Find out what it is like to be dissatisfied and not indulge it, not that there is anything wrong with fun and pleasure. Dissatisfaction, itself, is an exotic land to be explored, not for the purpose of getting rid of the dissatisfaction but because dissatisfaction is so rich, so amazing, so unexpected. Instead of trying to fix dissatisfaction when it arises, what about exploring it? The joy is always in the exploring, not where it takes you.

* * *

My tendency is that when I'm alone I can experience what you are talking about but when I'm with people I think I need to create drama or I don't have anything to talk about.

Sometimes when you are here in the moment, it's just a bunch of sensations. It's very ordinary.

Ordinary feels threatening. It feels like it's not okay.

Can you sense how that is a place where you can never rest? If ordinary is not okay, then life becomes a lot of work. Is ordinariness really so dangerous or horrible?

Sometimes I confuse ordinary with boring. Boring is not okay—unless I stop resisting it.

Are the sensations of boredom really so bad, if you don't set boredom against excitement? Life has both. When you really show up for boredom, you discover all the other qualities of being that are flowing in and out of that experience. But if you turn away from boredom and immediately pick up the TV remote, then you never find out if what I'm saying is true about boredom, although you may know that that richness is true of other kinds of moments, like exciting or blissful ones. When you are willing to show up for both the surface of your life and the depths, you'll find that the surface and the depths are not separate. When you show up for the boredom, it suddenly has all of the depth of your being in it.

* * *

Very often I choose to suffer. There is a point where I can choose suffering or not, and I choose to suffer. I think I have an addiction to suffering. Then later I feel sad over having chosen the suffering because I know I'm able to say no and follow the truth instead.

Even after some very deep insights, we may still choose to suffer. One of the reasons we do this is that it's easier because it's familiar, whereas staying in the experience of seeing the truth, at first, requires that we actively choose to not do what is easiest for us to do. This requires a lot of strength and presence.

Yes, because for me it's easier to suffer than to not suffer.

It is easier. It stinks, but it is easier. When you do choose not to do what will result in suffering, it can feel like a burning. Staying present to something you used to try to get away from can be very intense. It can seem like a wall of flames stands between you and the truth. What you've been avoiding seems like something terrible, but the wall of flames turns out to be very thin. It is easy to go through, but if you hesitate, you'll get burned. It will be horrible for those moments when you are half in and half out. But at some point, you are willing to go through the flames, and you discover that what you have been running from is not so bad. In fact, the truth feels very satisfying.

In the meantime, get really curious about the times when you choose to suffer. Really be present to that experience. If you really show up for the suffering, it will ruin it for you. You'll see that it's not worth it. The bad news is that suffering is what wakes us up. The good news is that suffering wakes us up. Eventually you reach a point when you are willing to just stay right here and look at the truth.

PART 8

Awakening

I may think I feel love
but it is love that feels me
constantly testing the woven fibers
that enclose and protect my heart
with a searing flame
that allows no illusion of separation

and as the insubstantial fabric of my inner fortress
is peeled away by the persistent fire
I desperately try to save some charred remains
by escaping into one more dream of passion
I may think I can find love
but it is love that finds me

meanwhile, love becomes patient and lies in wait
its undying embers gently glowing
and even if I now turn and grasp after the source of
    warmth
I end up cold and empty-handed
I may think I can possess love
but it is love that possesses me

and finally, I am consumed
for love has flared into an engulfing blaze
that takes everything
and gives nothing in return
I may think love destroys me
but it is love that sets me free

Awakening and Freedom

Awakeness is an innate quality of who you are. What we call "awakening" is recognizing not only that there is awakeness present but that that is who you are. At some point, you recognize the immense limitless perfection and innate awakeness of your true self. This happens on its own with no effort on your part. Spiritual awakening is similar to the recognition that you are awake in the morning after sleeping. All of a sudden you realize that you are awake, the sun is up, and it is time to get up. In the morning, you do not *do* anything to awaken. When the time is right, it just happens. Spiritual awakening also just happens when the time is right.

One of the dilemmas that many find themselves in is that they want to awaken more than life itself and yet they can do absolutely nothing to make that happen. The desire to awaken and the fact that you can do nothing about it are two immovable truths, which crush "you" between them. When you just rest in the place where you admit both of these truths, something indescribable can happen. When you just stay there and don't turn away just because the situation is impossible, then these two truths can wear away all of your mistaken ideas and illusions. What remains is an empty spaciousness that allows the truth of your being to become obvious. You still haven't done anything, but everything else has fallen away, leaving a clear space for the truth.

There is a difference between awakening, which is recognizing the truth of who you are, and Freedom, which is the end of suffering. Awakening is a gift of grace. That's the part that you can do nothing about. You can't do anything to make awakening happen. It just arrives, and it's not up to you when. However, Freedom comes as soon as you stop resisting what is happening or grasping after what is not happening. When you do that, the end to suffering is instantaneous. Freedom does not depend on awakening. What it depends on is wanting Freedom more than anything else—more than you want to maintain the illusion of a separate self.

After awakening, there is a natural reduction in the tendency to grasp or resist and therefore a reduction in suffering. However, even after awakening, the tendency to grasp can still arise, usually in more subtle ways, such as trying to hold on to the experience of awakening or longing for that experience to return. When that happens, suffering reappears. The good news is that Freedom is available in every moment—before, during, and after awakening— whenever you surrender your grasping and resistance. By surrendering your futile effort to change *what is*, you can be free. This choice to surrender is, in fact, the only true choice you have, since you can't choose to awaken. Then, as always, awakening will take care of itself.

Going Deeper Into the Truth

The movement of life is like a pendulum, swinging back and forth between what we label good and bad. We are intrigued by this movement and give it our attention. After a while, though, we sense there is more to life than trying to get the pendulum to swing a certain way or to remain in one place. Our efforts have never worked anyway and only resulted in struggle and suffering.

Then, by luck or by grace, we come across a deeper truth, which is that our happiness depends more on our attitude about what is happening than on what is happening. This is a central message in New Age and self-improvement circles. When you realize this, you drop to a deeper level of truth, where it doesn't matter as much whether things are going great or not; you can ride out the pendulum without it affecting your equilibrium or well-being. In this deepening, is a kind of transcendence of the problem of trying to make your life turn out right because that is no longer as important as once thought. In this deepening, another duality is often created, however: remembering the importance of attitude, and forgetting that. Or something happens that exceeds the capacity of your new perspective to handle, and you are caught in suffering again.

Finally, a willingness to look even deeper arises. What often accompanies this is the recognition that everything is God and therefore perfect, which makes the movement of the pendulum irrelevant. If it is all God, then it doesn't matter if it is, for instance, God with a lot of money or God with a little money. Your perspective shifts once again to a deeper, more inclusive truth, which ends much of the suffering and struggle and brings tremendous freedom. However, confusion and suffering can still be present in this perspective because there is still a "me" experiencing how perfect it all is. A new duality, or pendulum, has been created between seeing that it is all God and forgetting that it is all God.

The possibility is to go even deeper, to see that you *are* that perfection. You see not only that everything is God but that that is who you are. This shifts the perspective once again. When we speak of "becoming awakened," it is this shift in identity that we are referring to. All of the old frames of reference for identity—the body, the mind, the feelings—no longer apply. This truth now becomes your frame of reference, the place you look out from.

Although there is a huge dropping away of much of the suffering after seeing this, everything that was part of the first pendulum still exists: your body doesn't go away, the world doesn't go away, the rent doesn't go away. The pendulum is still swinging. It keeps cranking out this thing called experience and life. This doesn't change once you see the Truth, but seeing the Truth frees you from suffering over what you once suffered over. Often, we imagine that spiritual transcendence takes us beyond worldly concerns, but it simply means that more of the truth is included in our understanding of the world.

Each level you drop to is more liberating than the last. What allows this free-fall into deeper and deeper truth is letting go of trying to affect where the pendulum is. Finally, either from seeing the futility of your struggle, from pure exhaustion, or through grace, you let go and let the pendulum go wherever it will. Curiosity, along with stopping the effort, allows you to continue dropping into ever deeper truths. You no longer turn away from the next insight or try to hang on to the last one. You let yourself fall continuously into more and more truth. When you stop grasping or holding, the natural gravity of your being pulls you off the current apparent duality or pendulum and deeper into the truth of your being.

Somewhere along the way, we got the idea that there is somewhere to land, but that's not it at all. Each deepening just creates a new pendulum swing to then drop off of into further deepening. You are in a continuous free-fall into not knowing, where there is no suffering and many wonderful things happen. There is no end to the discovery of even deeper and deeper aspects of this Mystery. This deepening is actually the most natural thing in the world; it is your innate nature.

Life After Awakening

There is often an expectation that an awakening ends the tendency to identify and therefore to suffer, but this tendency continues even after awakening. Those who have had an awakening are often very surprised to discover this. The ego is not necessarily obliterated by a spiritual awakening; it just becomes more subtle. Nevertheless, there *is* a tremendous falling away of this tendency after an awakening. Many of your identifications are weakened or swept away by what you have realized, and you can't grasp in those directions any more. Although you might identify for a moment, you can't really buy the old stories anymore.

However, many find themselves grasping on to the awakening itself. They try to hang on to the expanded state that accompanied the awakening and make that into a new identity. Most of you have probably experienced this arising of spiritual ego either in yourself or others as pride in being someone who is awake. Another expression of this tendency to fixate is the experience of having reached Emptiness and it just being empty—boring. If you stop at any depth of awakening and try to hold on to it, it can quickly become lifeless or boring.

What is this tendency to attach an identity or grasp on to positive experience, including experiences of awakening? It is obvious that it is fed by conditioning, but conditioning is not the whole story. Identification or grasping is a capacity of Consciousness, itself, and not something we need to root out or fix—nor can we. It is Consciousness that engages in this illusion that it is a body or a feeling or an idea. After awakening, Consciousness often falls into the trap of identifying with the truth it has seen: "I am limitless Awareness."

All we can do when this tendency appears is to meet it with compassion and not turn away from whatever is arising, including grasping. All this requires is neither denying nor indulging in whatever feeling or reaction is arising. You just stay present to it and get curious about this tendency to fixate. Where does it come from? Find the source of it. From the beginning, it has all been an incredible play of Consciousness. There is no mistake in any of this. There is such richness in both the covering over of the Truth— the illusion—and the uncovering of it.

Something else that doesn't change after awakening is the amount of unhealthy conditioning you have. You inherited a certain amount of unhealthy conditioning, and that needs to be met. In meeting the unhealthy conditionning with an open, loving embrace, you can see the truth of the situation and become free from the misunderstandings that others passed on to you. The only difference after awakening is that you are willing to clearly see the truth of your conditioning and therefore you do not pass it on to others. In this way, you truly set free the conditioning or misunderstandings so that no one else ever suffers from them.

It is unrealistic to expect your conditioning to end once you have seen through the illusion "me." You may have inherited an unusually large bundle of conditionning. That's the relative world, the world of karma. For whatever reason, some people have very happy childhoods and some have very difficult ones. The amount of conditioning you have is not your fault. Besides, if this illusion is seen through, then the idea of any conditioning being "yours" doesn't even make sense. In truth, it isn't your conditioning at all.

Having a big bundle just means that you can be of even greater service because, if you set a big bundle free, then you have saved the world from a lot of suffering. And when you are done with that bundle, you can set other bundles free. At a certain point, you even find yourself getting excited when a contraction arises: "Ah, what's this one? What's underneath this?"

Bodhisattvas are individuals in the Buddhist tradition who forego liberation for the opportunity to set free more of the suffering of the world: they go back down into "hell," but with full awareness and love. Even if you could be done with "your" bundle of conditioning, there is a whole world of conditioning to be set free. You will never be done. It turns out that setting conditioned illusion free and uncovering the truth and beauty underneath is the greatest joy on earth. You become a slave to uncovering the Truth, but it's the best job you could ever ask for. So what if the pay is low!

The Point of No Return to Suffering

Everyone has had moments when the striving and struggling fall away, and the underlying happiness is revealed. Then, we go back into the world and get caught up in the striving and struggling again. Even after earth-shaking awakenings, this happiness, this peace, this recognition of the Truth seems to come and go.

You would think that after such glimpses, the world would no longer have its appeal; but that is underestimating the power of habit. We often fall right back into the old familiar habit of going back into the thoughts—the lies—that we call wanting, desiring, longing. When the mind has nothing to think about, it thinks about something it wants or doesn't want.

Rather than trying to stop an old habit, a useful approach is to replace it with a new one. When you are very busy with a new habit, you forget about the old one. The antidote to this most fundamental habit of believing we are someone separate, and the struggling and striving that result, is a new habit of looking and inquiring into what the truth is. However, it seems that it is not quite that simple. In a study with people who were trying to lose weight, it was discovered that techniques were not as important as reaching a point of feeling fed up with the struggle. Those who were successful said there was a point when they just said "enough." There comes a point when you have suffered enough over chasing after lies, and you can't do it anymore. You might still feel the urge, but it's no longer worth it, so you just live with the urge.

When you reach this threshold is not up to you, and there is no way of knowing where this point of no return to suffering lies. However, there *is* one very simple thing you can do to bring you closer to that threshold, and that is to be totally present in every moment, even to any suffering that may be present. When you are not present and, instead, you distract yourself with food, television, activities, drugs, or the like, you keep yourself away from that threshold. Fortunately, being aware of the present moment is actually the simplest thing you can do. Awareness is a natural function of being; you don't have to *do* anything. For example, is there anything you have to *do* to be aware of your hand? You just allow yourself to notice that awareness already includes your hand.

The invitation is to rest here in this Awareness and to be very present with whatever is happening, whatever is arising. We are so used to getting busy as soon as something is uncomfortable—or pleasurable. If it is uncomfortable, we get busy trying to fix it; and if it is pleasurable, we try to get it to stay or we try to get more of it. But if you simply stay present, then that which is aware—that which is seeing through your eyes and hearing through your ears— receives the full benefit and richness of that experience; and awakening will unfold on its own in ways that are guaranteed to amaze and surprise you. If you simply stay present even to the suffering that arises, this will bring you to the place of "enough," where you just can't play the game of wanting or desiring anymore.

Living the Truth

When anger arises lately, if I do give it words, there is a hollowness to it, like I'm going through the old motions of it. I think that is the step before not giving it words at all.

You know that it is not the whole truth even as you are saying it—the words taste funny as they are leaving your mouth.

Before that, when you're angry, there's such an agenda: there's self-righteousness and importance and your body heats up. But in the next stage, there is no physical reaction or any impetus behind the words. It's like saying the words in a play, like acting out a role. They are being spoken because they've been spoken so many times before, but there is no one behind them anymore—there are no guts behind them anymore. Then, it's hard to stay interested in those feelings anymore.

It's like a badly acted movie. You don't have to wait until the acting is that bad, though. Even when the body is heating up and the emotions are grabbing you, if you are willing, you can see that it is acting. You don't have to wall yourself off from those feelings; just be willing to see who or what is heating up. Who or what is noticing this acting job? Why wait until your acting gets bad—until it feels hollow? Just notice how even the most intense emotions have this emptiness underneath them.

And if you look, you will even find a hollowness at the core of joy and bliss and peace. The tendency is to try to improve the script—to write out anger and write in joy and other positive emotional states in their place. However, in the end, if these feelings also are believed, they just become part of another story: "I have arrived because I am happy all the time." For a while, it might be fun, but the hollowness will still be there because it is a lie.

Anything that comes and goes—joy, happiness, anger, sadness— can't be the whole truth of who you are. This hollowness at the core of every emotion and thought is a wonderful gift because it points to something truer. Telling the whole truth is admitting that this hollowness is here, even when your body is heating up or you are swept away with joy and bliss. The hollowness comes from the idea that it is "your" happiness, "your" bliss, or "your" anger.

The tricky thing about awakening is that a new identity is born. The new identification is with being blissful, happy, and spiritual because "you" are awake.

Yes. If you go deeper, you realize that you can't take any credit for that happiness and bliss. When the script takes a turn for the better, you can't take credit for it. You don't get the credit anymore, but you also don't get the blame anymore either, not even for this obnoxious spiritual personality that shows up. It's not your fault. All of this self-judgment is a waste of time because there is no one that it applies to.

Even spiritual experiences have this hollowness at their core. The purpose of a spiritual experience is not to solve your problems or make "you" enlightened. Spiritual experiences come and go, and that is all you need to learn from them. When you discover that even profound spiritual experiences leave you feeling hollow, then you are left truly naked in this Mystery.

Freedom for Whom?

I was reading an article recently about how the wealth recently gained in the stock market has affected some people. The article pointed out one of the dangers in the freedom created by a sudden influx of money into someone's life, which is in becoming indulgent. This was a very wise observation. The problem arises because the freedom is being put at the feet of something personal. It's being adopted by the "me," which is like pouring gasoline on a fire. Whatever is present in that story "me" flares up. Any tendency that exists flares up and can become addictive, whether it is a tendency to indulge in drugs or sex or material possessions or anything else.

As I was reflecting on this, I realized the beautiful parallel to what we call spiritual freedom. If an experience of the truth of who you are is put in service to the "me" ("I have awakened. I know the truth."), that is like pouring high-octane gasoline on any remaining tendency to grasp. In the wake of self-realization, suffering can re-appear if the truth that is discovered—that there is no personal self—is put aside and the joy, bliss, and freedom that result from that recognition are co-opted by the "me" and put back into service to the separate self. If you put the results of your realization in service to the "me," it will only fuel the tendency to grasp. On the other hand, if you put the joy, bliss, and freedom in service to the Truth, then it fuels even deeper realization.

Many people have spiritual awakenings after everything falls apart because when nothing is going right, we are often willing to look deeper. The strange thing is that the same possibility exists when we finally get something we really want or get everything we want and discover we still aren't happy. Both getting what we want and not getting what we want can result in looking more deeply into life. When you do look more deeply, you find that there is something more fundamental than these superficial desires: the longing for Freedom, for the Truth.

Even the longing for Truth and Freedom has to burn itself out, however, just as with the longing for money or any other desire. One way this can happen is by having so many spiritual experiences that you finally realize they don't matter. No matter how beautiful they are, you are still left with the question: So what? Now what? The great blessing is that this same question can also show up when you are in what could be called a spiritual desert.

Just like it can show up when everything is going your way, it can show up when everything is not going your way, when everything falls away. These extreme situations seem to put things into focus.

When another spiritual teacher was here, I thought about following her from place to place just to stay in the bliss I experienced with her. After she left, I experienced a let down and some depression after all that bliss. I'd still rather be in the bliss than in the depression, but the bliss goes away eventually.

Wanting spiritual bliss is no different than wanting a million dollars. The underlying structure of wanting is the same. Wanting Freedom serves a purpose along the way. It's been likened to the stick that you use to stir a fire: when you are down to the coals, you throw that stick into the fire too. Wanting Freedom, or the Truth, results in your looking more deeply—beyond your superficial desires—but at a certain point, you have to look at that desire too, which is spiritual grasping, and see what that is all about. One way of investigating this is to ask: What is present both when the bliss is here and when it is gone? What is present now that has always been present?

Stillness.

Does it come and go or does everything else come and go in that?
Stillness seems to be discovered when there is a gap in the chaos of life. Even though stillness is always here, it is not always recognized.

What is present even when there is no recognition of stillness? It seems like something has been lost or hidden by the experiences of life, but what is present even amidst the cacophony of life? What is present both in silence and cacophony, that doesn't depend on silence or the absence of turmoil? A good place to look for it is right here, right now. What do you find right here and now

that has always been present even before you knew there was
something like stillness?

Presence.

Yes. That is here even when the cacophony is ridiculously
loud. The "problem" with Presence is that it is not personal. There
is nothing in it for "you." So, as long as there is still some desire
for things to be good for "me," you are likely to dismiss the
Presence and wish for something juicier like bliss or stillness.
However, bliss and stillness are just expressions of the Presence.
The Presence, itself, is not contained in any one of its expressions.
Presence is the source of the bliss and the stillness, and it is also
the source of the tumult.

Is Presence like the watcher?

Presence includes the watching *and* the cacophony *and* the
stillness. The watching also comes from this Presence, and it is
also very impersonal. If you try to make the Presence be only the
watching, a separation is created: I am the watcher.

(Another questioner) *For about a week and a half, it feels like I've been
suspended in the middle of this huge space. Is this space I'm experiencing what
you're calling Presence? I don't know what this is. My second question is: is
my desire to stay in the center of this space just another desire?*

Welcome to the club. No one knows what this is. It's too big
for knowing. Your second question is also interesting. Is this space
here right now?

Yes, very much so.

Can you find a boundary to it? Where is this place that is not
in the center of it?

When I start holding on to anything whatsoever, even a little bit.

Okay. Hold on to something right now. Where does it take you that is outside the center of this space?

It's not outside the space; it's just not in the center of the space. It's just that being in the center feels better, more pure. When I'm in the center, nothing matters.

What is present in both the center and the place that is off-center? What is present in both of these expressions of the Mystery? Is that place where nothing matters ever really absent?

Not when I notice. Not when I remember.

Is this all-inclusive Space where nothing matters an experience that you are having or is that who you are?

That's who I am.

If that is who you are and it is all-inclusive, then anything—even the feeling of centeredness—can come and go and it won't matter. But if you believe that this is an experience "you" are having, then its coming and going can seem like a problem. Once you realize that this is who you are, then these moments of feeling off-center can be viewed as opportunities to discover what you haven't seen about yourself yet. Then, you may even find yourself becoming excited whenever you feel off-center because of the opportunity to discover an even larger space, one that is so large that even this feeling of being off-center is seen as happening in the center of this larger spaciousness.

Rather than trying to protect this Spaciousness, there is a new question to ask: Is there any problem or misunderstanding that you can give this Spaciousness away to? The only way to really protect it is to give it away because when you are willing to give space to problems, misunderstandings, and uncomfortable feelings, you discover how truly vast and limitless the Spaciousness is. There is room in it for everything.

Liberation Through Facing Death

Tibetan Buddhism talks about death as being the true test of liberation. If you can be present with complete equanimity in the moments preceding death, the moment of death, and the moments following death, then your liberation is complete. You passed the final test. Everything up to that point was a dress rehearsal for that final test.

When Ramana was a teenager, he was struck with an overwhelming fear of death. In that moment, he was convinced that he was about to die, but rather than calling for help, he just laid down and experienced it with curiosity. He didn't die, but he went through the experience of death with the question: What is it that dies and what is it that does not die? If my body dies, and I still exist, then who am I? In realizing that he was not the body, he was then no longer troubled by what was happening to the body or in the mind or emotions. He was free of all of that. The beauty of this story is that it suggests that you don't have to wait until death to experience liberation. You can elect to take this test prior to the scheduled date! You can voluntarily find out what dies and what does not die.

The truth is that we are always dying, in every moment. Everything we know is already dead—it is old news. For instance, right now while we are sitting here, you don't really know if you have a house, although you knew it when you left home this morning. What you once knew is no longer true, at least not in the way you knew it. Even if your house is still there when you get home, it isn't exactly the same as when you left. The Mystery has moved on, and the knowing of this moment is not the knowing of the last moment.

This applies equally to "you." We do this amazing thing called forming an identity or self-image. We form our self-image out of all our dead memories, thinking that somehow this image can be a source of life, a source of truth. However, when you inquire into this, you find that who you thought you were is already dead; it is old news. If your self-image isn't living your life, then what is? Who or what is this mysterious thing called life? When we admit that our self-image is like a zombie that we animate with our mind— when we admit our own death, our own lack of existence—then what is left is life. What is left is an incredibly alive Presence.

Falling in Love

All we are talking about here is that blessed point in your life when, either through wisdom, maturity, or pure exhaustion with the alternatives, you finally fall in love with *what is*—you fall madly in love with things exactly the way they are. All of us have had moments of this—we've flirted with *what is*. Every now and then, we have given it a little loving attention. But the truth is that most of us have spent a lot of time chasing other lovers, and all those other lovers are, of course, *what is not*. They are our images, our constructs, our ideas. They aren't actually *what is*, and that is why they are such lousy lovers, why they are so unsatisfying.

The question is, Have you had enough yet of these lovers who have left you high and dry? Falling in love with *what is*, is a very mature kind of love. It's not always as glamorous as your fantasies. Everything else that you have ever been in love with has actually been either a fear or a fantasy. It's funny to talk about being in love with one of your fears; but if you are honest about how much time and attention you give your fears, there must be some kind of a love affair going on because that is what love is—giving attention to something. We've been doing that a lot with our fears and fantasies, so the invitation is to do it instead with *what is*.

An awakening is simply a moment of clearly seeing this lover. It is a moment when you see *what is* more completely. It's not surprising that when someone has had a profound awakening, they often fall madly in love with *what is* because it is a rich and beautiful reality.

Some of you may have had the experience of working along side of someone for years and then finding yourself on a patio at a party under the stars falling in love with this person. You didn't realize until then how amazing this person was. That is the gift of an awakening: you suddenly see the beauty that was there all the time. This is a nice metaphor because, after that, you have a whole range of experiences together that aren't at all like that first night on the patio when you fell in love.

The point of that first night was not to find a way to live the rest of your life on the patio talking with your beloved nor is the point of an awakening to keep the experience of awakening forever. The point was what it allowed you to see. Then, the question is, Are you willing to carry through after seeing that? Are you willing to be in love with what you saw? The purpose of an awakening is to give birth to this mature love—this love for *what is*. We all have had moments of clearly seeing the beauty that was there all along, but do we pick up the phone the next day and "call" the truth back? Or do we go chasing after another dream lover, another fantasy? Many have awakenings but never go out for a second date.

You also may have had times when falling in love has happened more gradually. Awakenings are not the point, and they are not even necessary. You can fall just as deeply in love with *what is* without an awakening. The good news is that you don't have to *try* to fall in love with *what is*, which doesn't work anyway. All you have to do is notice that love is here already. You don't have to get rid of your fears and fantasies; just notice that love is also present, flowing even toward them. Once you recognize this, then your fears and fantasies lose their importance. There is no longer any need to protect against your fears or satisfy your fantasies because now you are in touch with the love, which those had been in service to. Then, anything that arises is seen as an opportunity for the recognition of love.

You don't have to *do* anything to fall in love with *what is*. How do you *do* falling? This falling in love is what has been happening all along. All of your sordid affairs with fears and fantasies have been in service to your being ready for this mature love; there has been no mistake and there is no penance to pay. All you have to do is recognize this love that exists in every moment. Whether as a result of an awakening or from maturity or from exhaustion with the suffering of falling in love with a fantasy, at some point, you throw your heart open to *what is*. You fall into the easiest place to fall, which is right here, right now.

This *what is* that I am talking about is the perfect lover— beyond your wildest dreams. It is completely devoid of jealousy. You can chase after all your fears and fantasies for years, and when you turn around, there it is just waiting for you. You've just slept with everyone else in the universe, and all it says is, "wasn't that sweet."

I'll give you an example from my own life of what it's like to fall in love with *what is*. The other night, I missed the chance to earn 600 frequent flyer miles because I forgot to use the right credit card. All night long, the thought kept coming up: "damn!" So, then I decided to look at that experience of being angry with myself. It's only human that, at first, we look at it because we want it to go away. I did that a couple of times, and then a half hour later, the thought was still coming up. So, finally, I just let myself get into that feeling of "damn!" and then I realized what fun I was having— no wonder I kept doing it! Once I saw that, I just fell in love with being angry with myself. I saw how beautiful it was. I finally saw what a rich experience it was. Now I just laugh if that feeling comes back. It doesn't matter now if it goes away or if it comes back a thousand times because I've fallen in love with it. It's sweet.

I'm not talking about falling in love with *what is* if that is not what is happening. If right now, you are in love with one of your fears, then just fall in love with that experience of closing down, hiding, protecting, fearing. Find out what that is all about if that is what's happening because you don't get to choose which *what is* you are experiencing right now. If you are longing right now for something better to come along, just notice how rich that experience of longing is, how beautiful it is, how worthy of love it is—before you've fixed it or gotten rid of it or talked yourself out of it. Fall in love with that. *What is*, along with being the perfect lover, is also a master of disguise. It puts on different disguises. It puts on the disguise of your own fear or longing. All it is waiting for is for you to say, "Oh yes, there you are my beloved. What a beautiful disguise!"

When you fall that deeply in love, what you find out is that it is not a personal love. The only way you can fall in love with something as vast and varied as this master of disguise is to fall right out of yourself. This body/mind isn't a big enough container for that much love. The only thing big enough for that much love is something very large and impersonal.

Commitment to Truth

The beginning of the end of a relationship is often when the subject of marriage or living together comes up. The same thing can happen when there is a glimmer of recognition that there is no "I." There is often a tendency to distract oneself or get busy, to somehow avoid this that is always present. As in a relationship, we are not always willing to go a little deeper.

When there is a glimmer of the Truth, the natural tendency is to run. Many spiritual seekers run from teacher to teacher looking for *their* teacher. After doing this for a while and hearing each teacher point to the Truth, *your* teacher is the one you stay with long enough to go where he or she is pointing instead of running on to the next teacher. It's not that that teacher is more special than the rest, he or she is just the one you stay with long enough to overcome your resistance to realizing the Truth. So, the invitation is to stay here in the Truth.

Just as in a relationship there comes a point when you are willing to stay even when the fear of commitment is stirred up, there comes a point in spiritual seeking when you realize that, at any cost, you are willing to stay. Often, the reason for running in a personal relationship is the potential for loss—what was "mine" becomes half "yours." In recognizing the deeper truth that there is no "you," you don't lose just half; you lose it all. You have to be willing to let go of everything that came before, or at least your investment in it.

If there is no more "you," then who decides to stay?

The paradox is that, in spite of everything I just said, you still wake up in the morning and decisions need to be made—where to go on vacation, whether to stay in a relationship, whether to give your life to the Truth in this moment. *Apparent* decisions are part of the unfolding of every moment. The difference is where you put the credit. "You" have never made a single decision, and yet choosing has been happening. All along, the Mystery has been choosing through "you."

* * *

I've often suggested that you give Truth the same quality of attention that you would a new lover: be willing to stay present to everything. There is an even deeper possibility: marriage to the Truth. Just as there comes a point when you have had enough love affairs, there comes a point when you are ready for a more committed, deeper involvement with the Truth.

There is a wonderful fairy tale about a princess who meets up with a frog who tries to talk her into kissing him. Finally, out of the goodness of her heart, she kisses the frog, and it turns into

Prince Charming. To be honest, marriage to the Truth can feel like you are agreeing to marry a frog.

The sacrifice that is called for is giving up your idea of yourself, or the illusion of being a separate self. Despite all the entertainment value that this illusion has provided, it has been the source of all of your suffering, all of your struggle, and all of your problems. You have to be willing to give everything up—your possessions, your roles, your dreams, although these things may or may not be lost.

You have to be willing to kiss the Truth even though it may look like a frog and have some incredible warts.

There is one catch: even when you have kissed the frog, there is no telling when it will turn into a prince. So, you just stay *here*; you just stay present. People used to ask my teacher, Neelam, "How long do I need to stay present?" She would reply, "As long as it takes." The invitation is to find out what happens if you just stay present to this endless Mystery, whether it takes a day or a year or a lifetime.

* * *

a lasting marriage
when devotion has claimed you for its own
no longer any chance to stray
a brief fling with illusion no longer satisfies
the truth demands utter fidelity
with no possibility of divorce
all pain must be faced
and embraced as the true countenance of your beloved
all fear must be met
and recognized as the thrill of tasting the unknowable
all joy must be surrendered
and acknowledged as a gift with no giver
this union only requires telling the truth
even when the truth shatters your dreams

even when the truth leaves you emptied out
even when the truth reveals your counterfeit existence
then there is no other possibility
            than happily ever after

PART 9

Living Life as a Question

Your hands have a cool dry touch
And yet they warm my heart
Your eyes are emptier than the night sky
And yet they pierce my defenses
Your body does not even exist
And yet you dance so beautifully
That I am lost in tears

How can silence say so much?
How can empty space feel so full?
Chasing after more and more is so futile
When only less will satisfy

Living Life as a Question

Many of the questions and concerns in satsang come in a similar form: How do I get or keep a particular experience? How do I get or keep a sense of awakeness or expansion or openness or freedom or loving kindness or Presence? Or if worldly concerns are the issue, the question is the same: How do I get or keep more health, more wealth, more comfort, more security, more romance? Another form these questions take is: How do I avoid falling asleep or feeling stuck or being contracted or being sick or losing love? They're good questions. There's nothing wrong with them. They're real for the person who's asking them.

Within each of these questions is the assumption that you need to do something—you need to get or keep or avoid something. Right there, in that assumption, is our suffering. The effort to get or keep or avoid any experience is what makes life miserable, difficult, dis-easeful.

In satsang, another possibility is pointed to, a way of touching your experience without either trying to hold on to it or push it away. It's a way of reaching out to your experience and really seeing what's it's like. In doing this, the questions become: How open or stuck am I right now? How open or closed is my Heart right now? How happy or sad am I right now?

And when the answer comes, the question becomes, What's that like? What's it like to be expanded or contracted or whatever it is you are experiencing? What's it like to have an open Heart or to not be in touch with your Heart at all in a particular moment? What's it like to be filled with love? What's it like to feel a lack of love? This is reaching out and touching the experience as it is and as it naturally changes. It's not a static question, but an alive one; you're never done with that question.

In doing this, rather than trying to change life, you're living life *as* a question. What's this like? And what's it like now that I've noticed what this is like? And what's it like now? And now that it's changed again, what's it like? Even your noticing something changes it, so by the time you've found an answer, it's time to ask the question again.

We've been so conditioned to think that the point of questions is to get answers that we overlook that the point of answers is that they get us to more questions. The questions are as valid and rich as any answer because every answer is full of questions. You can even begin to enjoy the questions, even trust the questions, as much as any answer that comes.

When you value the questions themselves, you just naturally hold the answers more lightly because they aren't the goal. If the question is just as rich as the answer, then it's fine if the answer comes and goes. Have you ever noticed that you've forgotten everything you once understood? Every insight you've ever had has faded, and that's great because then you're back in the question. You're back in this really alive place where you're getting to find out what you know now, what's happening now, what's moving, what's changing, what it's like now. What is it like now? You'll never be done with that question. What's happening now? You could say that answers are just a temporary side effect of having questions.

This is a gentler, more respectful way of being with your experience. It's a more intimate way of being with your experience every moment to ask what it's like instead of How can I fix it? How can I get more? How can I get less? How can I improve it? How can I change it? How can I avoid it? How can I hang onto it? Do you see how all of these questions have an effort to them? They have a sense of violence to them—a sense of being in battle with or in opposition to your life. It's hard to be intimate with someone when you're pushing them out the door or trying to keep them from leaving. There's no intimacy in that kind of interaction. How much possibility is there for real, deep contact? The same thing is true for other dimensions of our Being. The opportunity is to intimately experience the expansions and contractions, the openings and the closings, the freedom and the stuckness, the wonder and the confusion, the understanding and the lack of understanding.

So, what question is moving in you right now? No matter what that is, that's the place to start because that's what's moving in you right now. If a desire is moving in you right now, what's it like to want something? Or if it's a fear, what's it like to fear something? There are no wrong questions; they're all entry points, places where this inquiry can open up and become soft and intimate. So, what's moving in you right now?

Self-Inquiry

Beyond focusing on the content of our experience and even beyond noticing whether we're expanded or contracted, a wonderful question is: "Who or what is experiencing this?" This is a variation of the classic self-inquiry question, "Who am I?"

As I was going through my email the other day, I ran across a quote from *A Course in Miracles* that essentially said that you'll never find satisfaction in the world. This assertion is at the core of most spiritual teachings. Spiritual teachings and practices attempt to turn us in another direction, away from the usual places we look for satisfaction. They're designed to shift our focus from the world of form to Beingness. Self-inquiry is one technique for doing that. In self-inquiry, we simply ask, "Who am I?" or "What am I?" or a variation on that: "Who is having this experience??

When you look to see who is having this experience, you don't find anyone. There's nothing there. The Experiencer can't be experienced, just as the eye can't see itself. You don't find any *thing*, nothing you can touch or see or hear.

When *nothing* is discovered, people often keep looking instead for *something* they think they're supposed to find. It's only natural to look somewhere else when you don't find anything. We don't expect that *nothing* is the answer. So we go back to our mind for the answer—we think about it, check in our memory, or imagine a good answer—instead of just staying with the question. But inquiry done only with the mind is dry—it lacks juice. After a while, because this experience is not very rich, the mind often gets bored and quits. There isn't much in it for the mind.

Another way to ask the question is with your whole Heart. You ask it with everything you've got, as if your life depended on it. If you ask the question with this kind of passion and intensity, it will bring you beyond what the mind is able to figure out. When you ask it with your whole Heart and you don't find an answer, you just stay there, not knowing. You just let yourself not know. There's nothing but that space, and you just stay present to that space, to that sense of there being nothing behind your eyes, nothing behind your thoughts, nothing behind your feelings. Instead of turning back to thing-ness when you don't find anything, you just stay there in the no-thing-ness and get curious about it. Nothing—what's that like?

In looking and finding nothing, what you discover is even more space. Staying with the question "Who am I?" opens up space. Nothingness is very spacious; there's a lot of room in it. When you stay in that nothingness, you discover that there's a lot of stuff in that space, stuff that is real in a way that the stuff in the world has never been real. What moves in that space are true qualities of Being, such as Love, Compassion, Insight, and Strength.

Every time you turn towards Beingness, a different quality shows up. Being has an infinite number of qualities, which show up fresh and different in every moment. These qualities can seem to exist in another dimension, as they have a depth and solidity about them that is more real than physical objects.

These qualities have been there in the nothingness all along, and as you stay with the nothingness, they begin to be apparent. One way of staying with the inward focus is by repeatedly asking the question, "Who Am I?" Stay with the question even when you experience nothing and have no idea who you are. Just ask, "Who or what doesn't know?"

The Sense of Me

Nothingness with all of its qualities is present throughout every experience, no matter how beautiful or painful. Also throughout nearly the entire spectrum of experience, is a sense of *me*, of someone who is having an experience, although when you ask, Who is that? you can't find anything. Still, there is almost always a sense of identity, a sense of being, of existing. When you're contracted, there's still a sense of being, but it's a contracted sense of being. And when you're expanded, there's still a sense of being, but it's an expanded sense of being. When you're sad, it seems like *me* that is sad. When you're enlightened, it seems like *me* that is enlightened. When you drop a rock on your foot, it seems like *me* that is hurting. There's always a sense of a *me*.

Because there is so clearly a sense of *me* no matter what you're experiencing, there can be a tendency to try to manage or control that experience. This makes sense because it feels like your experience: *I* am having this experience, so *I* should be able to fix it or make it better. That is our suffering. Our suffering isn't really caused by this sense of *me* that is always present. That actually makes sense—everything that you experience *is* you. It's all you. Rather, our suffering is caused by the effort to try to change whatever we're experiencing. When *I* am having a painful experience, it seems like *I* need to do something about it. Even if *I* am having a good experience, *I* have the problem of figuring out how to keep it.

There are two ways to get out of this suffering. One is by asking the question, Who is having this experience? and realizing that you are nothing. Every time you ask this, the sense of *me* lessens and the sense of nothingness increases. There's still a sense of *me*, but there's less *me* and more nothing. This realization reduces suffering because there's less *you* that you have to manage and more nothingness, which doesn't require any management. Nothingness is low maintenance.

The other way out of suffering is the opposite realization: to realize that you are everything. You just notice that everything is *you*: That ceiling fan is *me*, that painting is *me*, and on and on. Just as there's no limit to how little *you* can become in the face of nothingness, there's no limit to how big *you* can become—to how much you can realize is *you*. When you are all the happiness and all the sadness in the world and all the money and all the poverty in the world, very little management is required. There's very little to do about it. And so, this realization eliminates suffering.

We could think of the first way of overcoming suffering as Inquiry and the second as Bhakti, the devotional path, in which you merge with everything. With Bhakti, rather than realizing you are nothing, as in Inquiry, you give your sense of identity to everything: I am that, I am that, and that too.

As beautiful as the realizations of nothingness and everythingness are, they don't necessarily touch the human. That's why when you wake up the next morning, there's still the sense of a limited *me* again. Because suffering happens in the arena of our humanness, many would like to know how to be done with the humanness. The point is not to fix or eliminate your humanness but to *realize* your humanness. This is done by asking, What is the humanness like today? What has the sense of *me* landed on today? The only way to liberate your humanness is to find out what's really true about the human experience.

The good news in all of this is that there's nothing you should avoid realizing. If right now you're experiencing something very human, that's exactly right. And if you're experiencing something transcendent, that's exactly right too. Your life has really been one long realization. Has there ever been a moment when you haven't been realizing something? Even when your sense of *me* is very small, you're realizing your *me*-ness. Sometimes our realizations are very human, very mundane. You don't have to wait for a particular realization to be realizing something.

Am I?

Inquiry is the practice that's offered in the tradition I come from. Inquiry is a way of exploring our experience and our Being. There are many possible questions. The granddaddy of them all is the question Who am I? One thing that has always bothered me about that question is the presupposition that I am a who—I am a somebody. The question *What* am I? is a little more open to other possibilities, but there's still a presupposition that I am some *thing*.

So, lately, I've been playing with stripping that question down to the question Am I? and noticing what that's like, what discovery that allows. This question not only eliminates presuppositions but brings the questioning down to something very fundamental, which is the simple fact of our existence. And yet in exploring this, it turns out that this is not such a simple fact; our existence is a profound mystery. The question also could be rephrased as Do I exist? If the question is kept this simple, then the answer is always in the affirmative—there is existence here. I am. But it gets dicey if you start adding anything to it.

This question Am I? points to the simple fact that you *are*, regardless of what you are experiencing. Beneath everything that's going on, is a sense of existing. This question points to a dimension other than experience.

Once that sense of existence is in your field of awareness, then it's possible to find out what's true about your existence, to explore that. What's it like right now to just be? Is it enough right now to just exist? Or is there a sense that it's not enough? All our lives we've been told it's not enough: You have to be smarter, richer, prettier, more enlightened, more compassionate, more loving, and on and on. You have to be some *thing*.

We have the sense that if we could just be what we're supposed to be, then we could just *be*. Take a fantasy about being richer, for instance: What's great about being richer is that you think it will finally allow you to just *be* because you no longer have to become richer. We think that being richer or smarter will finally allow just *being* to be enough. Wherever this inquiry takes you, it's amazing to discover both the extent to which our existence is enough and the extent to which we think it isn't.

For most, this sense of existing is associated with the body. Existing seems to happen there. However, does your sense of existence stop where your body stops? Discover for yourself where your experience of *I am* is right now. Is it in the body or is the body in it? Would it be more accurate to say "I exist in the body" or "the body exists in me"? Be willing to hold the possibility that who you are goes beyond the body even if you aren't experiencing that directly right now. The experience of the body never goes away, but the link between the *me* and the body can soften or dissolve when "I am the body" is seen as only part of the truth. If you experience the *me* outside the body even a little, then the body can't be the whole truth of who you are.

Where does your sense of *me* stop? Right now, for instance, allow more of your experience of the room in. When you include in your awareness the energy and information that's flowing in and out of the body, is there a greater or lesser sense of *me*? What is more true, to say, "I exist in this room" or "this room exists in me"? When you include the totality of the room and beyond, are you more in contact with your *me* or less in contact with it? Most people find that the more they include in their experience, the larger their sense of *me*. When you ask these questions, you discover there's not such a clear-cut boundary to *me*.

Of course, this exploration doesn't have to stop with your body or with this room. Try sensing the reality of the surrounding city. Is there a greater or lesser sense of *me* when you do this? You can also ask the question: Do I exist in space or does all of space exist in me? Which feels truer?

Shifting Your Reference Point

Your reference point—the *I* or the *me*—naturally expands and contracts. Sometimes it includes much more than our usual reference point—the body. We were taught to refer to what's happening in the body as *me,* but sometimes it also includes the room, the state, the country, the world, the whole universe.

You've probably had many experiences when the boundary of who you thought you were expanded and included more. Everyone has had such experiences, even if only as the result of something like a gorgeous sunset. These experiences bring a sense of just being able to hang loose—being able to let everything come and let everything go.

It's interesting to notice how variable this container called *me* is. Sometimes it's the body and sometimes it's even smaller than the body. Sometimes it's just your thoughts and ideas. What if it's totally arbitrary where this container of *me* ends? Does it have to end at the body? Does it have to be my body or my thoughts or my feelings or my desires that are *me?* Does that have to be the boundary?

There's a great exercise from speed reading that can give you a sense of what I'm talking about: Imagine holding a tangerine on top of your head and make that the point you're looking from. Then gradually let the tangerine float up three feet above and behind your head and imagine looking out from that point. You can even go farther out, as far as you can imagine. It's not that your senses will follow, but your perspective can shift to where you're sensing this moment from outside the universe. It's not that hard to do. And then you can bring it back down inside the body or down into your Heart. What's it like right now to look out from your Heart? Even that much of a shift, from the head down to the Heart, can profoundly alter your experience.

The point of this exercise isn't to show you the endless variety of states that are possible but to illustrate that what you usually think of as *me* has no real boundary. What does it mean if the boundary of the *me* is not so solid and defined? What if the container called *me* were bigger than this room or bigger than anything you can conceive? What would that change in your experience? You can see how it would take the edge off of everything: What sense would it make to struggle to move anything in or out of this particular location if that's not you?

If there is such a thing as a container for *me,* it's a very leaky one. No matter how narrow your reference point gets, it still won't hold still. No matter how deeply identified with your experience you are, your experience keeps changing. Have you ever noticed how love comes and love goes? Money comes and money goes? Experience comes and experience goes? Insight comes and insight goes? They move through this space, but they pay no attention to your ideas of *me* as the container, so you never successfully contain any of them. You never successfully hang onto anything. Everything just comes and goes. Everything just passes through.

The invitation is to get really curious about the truth of this container we call *me.* Does it contain anything? Can you find a definite place to put that reference point or does the reference point just naturally shift from moment to moment?

Self-Image vs. Reality

Accompanying our *experience* of existing, our sense of *I* or *me*, are lots of ideas about it. These ideas form into an image of who we are, commonly called a self-image. One way of exploring this experience of having a self-image is by asking: Am I happening in my image of myself or is my image of myself happening in me?

When faced with the greater truth of who we are, our more limited self-image and the ideas connected to it lose their power and significance because a lesser truth loses its sense of truth and impact in light of a greater truth. A simple example is Santa Claus: When you discovered the greater truth that Santa Claus is a myth, the experience of Santa Claus didn't go away, but the idea of Santa Claus had less power and significance to you. The point of this exploration is not to get rid of your self-image but to create the space for directly experiencing it or, moreover, for being what you truly are and allowing that to affect your image in whatever way it will.

Our self-images or identities aren't bad, and sometimes they're functional. For instance, to communicate "I'm a teacher" can be functional; it transmits some information. But in comparison to just being what you are in this moment, these more limited identities don't have much juice, much aliveness. To get your identity from a self-image is a dry and unsatisfying experience.

Another quality we assign to the *me* is stability. We're conditioned to think of ourselves as static images. Whenever we speak the words "I am," we are assuming a static reality. For example, "I am a doctor" or "I am a mother" implies a fixed reality, but of course, even these things change. Our self-images are attempts to create a stable, continuous idea of the self. And yet, in your actual experience, you find that your *me* is never the same way twice. It arises in every moment as something new and different. When you look, you discover that your *me* is more like a flow than a static object.

This ongoing flow is actually who we are. We are an ongoing flow of experience. Who we are isn't static, although our self-images are, and these images are either shaken by what's happening or reinforced by what's happening. We love it when our self-image is reinforced by what's happening; it's somehow reassuring, even if it's a negative self-image, because it allows us to pretend a little longer that the truth of who we are can be contained in a self-image.

Even so, it's only a matter of time before our self-image gets challenged. What we usually do then is switch to another one. We keep the illusion going of a static reality of ourselves by quickly changing self-images. Life has flowed into a new experience, and for a moment we're confused until we pull out a new image. Then we relax because we know who we are again.

Just try to notice both the ongoing flow that is present right now *and* this tendency to hold a self-image. It's one thing to become aware of the boundlessness and timelessness of existence and to lose awareness of the self-image, and it's another thing to bring awareness to both of these at the same time.

Does the sense of your self actually fit into any of your concepts about yourself? Can any of your ideas about yourself really capture this moment? How about the idea "I'm a spiritual seeker"? Can that really capture your experience right now? Or how about "I'm enlightened" or "I'm not enlightened"? Does that have any actual relevance to the experience you're having right now? Can any idea ever be a truer container for who you are than this ungraspable moment that's right here right now?

What does this mean if our existence is happening both inside and outside of all our ideas and images of ourselves? What happens when you simply allow both your images and your existence? Which one is the elephant and which one is the flea? It just makes sense that if you're in the presence of an elephant and a flea that you would pay more attention to the elephant. They're both present and they're both real, but if you're too distracted by the flea, you might miss what the elephant is doing.

Death

"Death" most often refers to the death of the form, but the experience of dying doesn't just happen when the body dies. Every experience you've ever had has died, and everything you're experiencing now is in its death throes. Of course, in every moment, there's also a birth—a new moment is being born. It's tricky to see this in the moment, but if you reflect back, you can see that everything that has come before is now dead and something new has taken its place.

This is a profoundly different view of how things happen than we're used to. Our concept of change is a misunderstanding: Reality isn't actually capable of change. Nothing ever changes; it can't. All it can do is die and be reborn. We think that something changes into something else. So, we go back and look at what happened before something changed to try to find the cause.

But that's not the way it happens. What really happens is that an old experience dies and a new one is born. There's no connection between what was and what is now, no cause and effect. In every instant, the universe that you know dies and a new one is born. Once you see this, time doesn't make sense anymore. There is no past that causes the present that causes the future. Life comes fresh each moment, completely unlimited by what came before. There's no telling what will be born in the next moment.

We can't see, for instance, how sadness changes into allowing because it never does. Sadness never becomes anything; it just comes to the end of its natural life. At some point it finally dies and something else unpredictable takes its place.

The question is, How willing are you to see that what is happening now in this moment has no relationship to the past? It's a little weird, and yet a lot of things suddenly make sense, such as why it rarely works out the way we expect when we to try to change something. One way of saying it is Being doesn't need to recycle. Being is limitless, so it just throws out the old and tries something new.

There's a powerful sense of a flow of time. It seems like the present is affected by the past, and the future is affected by what you do now. That illusion is really convincing. That's how good Being is at this game. But every now and then it throws out a whole new universe that doesn't at all correspond to what just was, and then we're left confused.

One of the ways this illusion gets maintained is through memory. Memory is the attempt to keep a dead moment alive. One way you see this is in a traumatic experience. In that moment, the experience seems to be too much, so rather than experiencing it fully, consciousness contracts and the experience goes into a memory or pattern of tension in the body. Because we weren't ready to be there completely with that experience, we put it aside, where it remained undigested. This strategy makes sense when you're a child and you don't have the resources to be with an experience.

Experiences like these need to be digested. Once you see that whatever traumatized you is no longer here and that you aren't a child anymore, you can handle looking at it. When you do this, you feel lighter. Anytime you let one of those dead corpses from the past go, you feel lighter. It doesn't need care and feeding anymore. What a relief. Trying to keep anything alive that's dead is a lot of work. No one has ever succeeded, even though we've all tried to keep some experience, some state, some perspective, some identity alive.

Every *me* that we've ever thought ourselves to be is like a zombie—the student *me* the adolescent *me,* the little boy/girl *me.* They're just corpses; there's no life in them. They're totally imaginary. So, how do you change or heal the child or adolescent *me?* The healing comes when you see that this *me* doesn't exist anymore; it's an imaginary corpse you were trying to animate and fix or an imaginary experience you were trying to animate and re-write. But when you check, you can't change it; it's dead—and naturally so.

This simple realization is the end of the problem. When you get up close enough to an experience, you see that it doesn't exist anymore. You see the truth of it—that it's no longer here, and that frees you from that particular illusion of cause and effect.

There are two ways to go about this. One way is to go directly to this moment, where nothing from the past exists. Meditation and inquiry are both designed to bring you to this place where nothing exists. Nothing exists because it's already dying by the time you notice that it's been born. That's how quick life is happening. When you come to that place, you realize that nothing's around long enough for it to exist and that nothing that ever happened still exists. That's the direct route, and it can dissolve all limitations in an instant.

The other approach is taking it bite by bite: You digest all that undigested experience. You work on your issues by bringing up those experiences. When you do this, it often feels like a burning. You experience an intensity, but now the experience doesn't exist, so no matter how intense it is, you can handle it. And then something weird happens, and the experience is no longer an issue. That something weird is that you realize that the experience doesn't even exist: You bit into something and found out that there's nothing there.

When you digest one of those experiences, you do feel lighter and something flows and your life gets better and your relationships get better because now there's room for that; you're not relating to the dead parent or the old spouse that was around yesterday but to whatever is being born in this moment.

The problem with this approach is that it fosters the illusion that all of this work on ourselves is going to do away with our problems. It can easily turn into an attempt to create a better *me,* one who never has a difficult experience, and that's not realistic. Besides, there's an endless supply of dead problems; new ones are being created every moment. So with this approach, you'll never be done. It's not that there's no place for this approach, but the point isn't to create a better *me* but to become free by arriving fully in this moment.

Shrinking Your Awareness Through Judgment

Spiritual practices and inquiry are means of opening up your awareness, of including more of the truth in your awareness. Even the simple practice of paying attention to your breath or to your body can expand your awareness and move your attention from the content of your thoughts to a larger context. Spiritual inquiry brings your awareness to the biggest context of all—what is awareness itself? What is it that is aware of whatever is going on?

Judgments, on the other hand, are a means of narrowing or closing down your consciousness or awareness. You could say they're the muscle we flex to contract our consciousness. When a judgment arises, you lose touch with your Beingness and suddenly feel very small. Judgments contract the sense of who you are, the sense of your self.

Most of us are very familiar with the many forms judgment takes: all the would-haves, could-haves, should-haves, and all the hopes, wishes, dreams, doubts, fears, and worries. We're all painfully familiar with the ongoing mental commentary about how things could have been better or could be better or should be better or will be better—or worse.

A judgment shrinks our attention onto the content of the judgment. We get caught up in the content and keep ourselves busy (at least mentally if not actually) trying to make life fit these judgments. Rather than being present to things the way they are, we're busy trying to make life be different than it is. When we're judging, our attention becomes narrowly focused on that, and we leave out much of the truth of the moment.

Contraction is really just another capacity of consciousness. The problem isn't with the narrowing of attention, which can be functional, but with keeping it there longer than necessary. At times it's useful to narrow your consciousness onto something like balancing your checkbook. But if, for example, there's a judgment about the figure you come up, you can spend a lot more time looking at your checkbook than is functional. Once you know there's only $.37 in your checking account, it's not useful to keep your attention focused on that. But it was functional to find out.

It is as natural for consciousness to contract as it is to expand. Whenever something appears in your awareness, consciousness naturally contracts onto it for a moment. For example, a bird flies in front of you and you naturally focus on it for a moment. If there's no judgment attached to that, then consciousness expands again and begins to take in more. However, any judgment or opinion about the bird, either positive or negative, will keep your attention narrowly focused on it. This may then spin off into a full-blown story about a bird or birds or other thoughts, which further keep your attention focused on a small portion of what's occurring in this moment.

We work very hard at our judgments. When a judgment hooks us, our minds spin around and around on that one thought. We give our judgments this much energy because we're convinced that they'll help us change our reality. We believe they have the power to change what is, but they only keep us discontent with what is.

Isometric exercises are a good metaphor for this: You contract your muscles against a wall but the wall doesn't move. You make a lot of effort, but it results in no movement, no change. That's what we experience in judgment—lots of ideas and struggle but no change in what is. Just having an idea about what's supposed to happen or not, doesn't change what's happening. In the midst of all of our struggling against it, life just happens the way it happens. All this struggling against life is futile. We suffer, but our suffering doesn't change what is.

Judgment takes a lot of effort. Keeping our attention this small takes a lot of effort because it goes against the nature of consciousness, which is to expand as well as contract. Because consciousness naturally expands, when we stop our effort and involvement with the content of our thoughts, we usually experience an expansion—a natural relaxation and broadening of our awareness. Some of us spend so much time in this effortful contraction of consciousness called judgment that even a slight relaxation of this effort can result in a profound sense of expanded consciousness.

This struggle against the natural flow of consciousness is our suffering. The good news is that there's no harm done to consciousness when it contracts. No matter how contracted you've been, consciousness never loses its capacity to expand. Once you realize that it's natural for consciousness to alternate between expansion and contraction, you can just allow it to move freely and enjoy the wonder of whatever state you're in.

It can be useful to distinguish between judgments and observations. A simple thought like "it's dark out" can be just an observation, and our awareness can for that moment include the fact that it's dark out and then go on to whatever else is happening. But if you're lost in the woods without a flashlight, this thought may take on the quality of a judgment, like "Oh no, this is dangerous," and your awareness contracts and suddenly you're less present to the situation.

Anything—the color of someone's pants, the electrical outlet, the temperature in the room—can be experienced as a simple observation or can trigger a judgment. Most of our experience passes as observation. We're actually only capable of having one judgment at a time. Most of what's in your experience right now is not a problem for you at all. Many more things register in your Being as neutral than as judgments.

Judgment has a payoff or we might not bother with it. Its real purpose is to narrow attention or awareness. When awareness becomes contracted or narrowed, unconsciousness expands. As our awareness gets smaller, what we're not aware of gets larger.

What is arising can be either good or bad, but it may be too intense, too threatening to your comfort or security, too uncomfortable to others who are present, or contrary to cherished beliefs. When that is the case, a judgment may arise to narrow your consciousness so that what you don't want to be aware of becomes unconscious.

Check this out for yourself: The next time a judgment arises, ask yourself what was coming up just before that. You will often find something that seems uncomfortable, and the judgment serves to temporarily contract your awareness off of the discomfort.

But there's a price: The price is a sense of restless unease, of never being at peace, because the natural tendency of awareness is to open and be aware of more. It takes effort to keep your consciousness in a narrow range. You can't completely relax, because the second you do, you notice all kinds of things that your judgments were keeping out of awareness.

This also happens with positive judgments. An example is when something profound shows up and you react with a positive judgment, such as "I'm having an incredible spiritual experience." This positive judgment narrows your attention onto a limited aspect of that experience, like how good it feels or how it might impress others, so that now most of what's going on is no longer in your awareness. When we feel an expansion of awareness, judgment often narrows the experience this way into something we can handle. Through your judgment you have shrunk it into a nice small manageable experience.

Judgment also serves the function of maintaining the sense of a separate *me* by shrinking the sense of who we are. Judgment keeps the sense of your self very small and manageable. The *me* only exists in the mind, and judgments are a way the mind maintains the idea of a *me*: I am someone who is good, who is bad, who is smart, who is dumb, who has a problem, who doesn't have a problem (fill in the blanks for yourself). These are the stories we tell ourselves, which create our identity and the sense of a separate self.

Judgment also creates a *me* by focusing the mind on a problem (i.e. an uncomfortable feeling or experience), which it then goes about trying to fix. So, judgment either serves to block out what is uncomfortable by narrowing our awareness or as a springboard for trying to fix whatever is uncomfortable. All of our curiosity becomes focused on changing our experience rather than simply allowing it and being curious about it. Our attention becomes focused on a fraction of what's going on.

We actually create problems (which stem from our judgments) because they give us an identity. They give our mind something to do. Our problems structure our lives. Now you know who you are and what you're going to do: I'm someone who has a problem and who has to solve that problem. That's who I am and what I'm going to do with my life. Now you have a story.

We think that judgment is about fixing our reality, but it's really about not experiencing our Being because our Being—in addition to being beautiful, profound, and satisfying—is a pretty wild thing. It doesn't always show up in a comfortable, safe, easy form.

This tendency to judge is not your fault. We learned to use judgment when we were very small. The judgments we received as children were attempts to manage the size and range of our Being. Early on, we were subject to a lot of judgments that were relatively effective at keeping our Being in check. We quickly learned what range of Being was acceptable. Every time we stepped outside that range, we got hit with a judgment from parents, teachers, siblings, or other figures in our life. Over time, we incorporated this strategy for managing this unruly thing called Being: You keep it under control and make it better by flooding it with judgments, both good and bad. Judgments were used by others and eventually by ourselves to shape and fit us into what was comfortable for those around us.

This function of judgment has sometimes served us very well. When you're little and you experience something abusive or tragic, it can be very functional to be able to narrow your attention so that you're not aware of your body anymore. However, because no one can keep this up indefinitely, painful memories that were once unconscious pop into consciousness. Everyone experiences this to some extent. Other things that we try to hold at bay with judgments are boredom, emptiness, and a sense of the ordinariness of life.

So you see, the experience of judgment is not really about the content of the judgment. That's why we often come up with the most ridiculous judgments. They can be very silly, and the absurdity of their content sometimes wakes you up out of them. Then usually the mind comes up with another judgment, one that you won't question. Unfortunately, unless we're really aware of what's going on with our judgments, once we see through the ridiculousness of one, we often come up with another to take its place until that one has worn us out.

The good news is that there's a limit to our capacity to judge. No one has ever managed to keep it up continuously. It's too much work to keep consciousness focused on a particular problem. Some of us get so good at it that it becomes habitual, but it's still a lot of work. When we finally do stop this effort, awareness naturally expands. When you're no longer concerned about the content of your judgments, your awareness opens up and includes more of what's going on. Suddenly, you notice that there's a lot more going on in the room, in your sensations, in your experience than what you had been focused on.

We might think that the antidote to judgment is some kind of spiritual technique that causes consciousness to expand, but since there is a built-in limit to how long we can stay focused on a judgment, the real antidote is simply to notice how often judgment fails. The default position of consciousness is actually to include more and more. Consciousness only contracts when there's a reason, whether it's to balance a checkbook or keep something unconscious.

Once we see the truth about judgments, the tendency is to want to rid ourselves of them, but that's just layering more judgment onto judgment. We can't keep judgments from arising. Another possibility is to really *experience* your judgment rather than focusing on its content. Just notice: What's it like when there's a thought about how things could be different or better or happier or less painful? You come to see how much effort judging is and how futile it is.

When you finally just stay with what you've been trying to avoid, you discover that what you've been avoiding is not really so bad. Consciousness can withstand the anger, boredom, sadness, fear, doubt, worry, and even a traumatic memory or experience—as well as bliss. You learn that you have a greater capacity than you thought for these things.

Once you experience how tiring resistance is and just allow yourself to experience whatever you're experiencing, then awareness naturally expands. When that happens, the experience you're having takes on a richness: You may feel sad, for instance, but it feels so good to feel the sadness that's here—because it's real. It's like discovering another dimension of experience, like being engrossed in a book and then suddenly noticing the birdsong that was there all along. So, the invitation is just to get to know your experience as it is.

Our fear is that if we experience these things, they'll overwhelm us. But when you just rest in the experience and don't go back to some surefire way of narrowing your consciousness, guess what happens? The sense of emptiness or anger or whatever becomes filled in with something truer, something with more depth to it. You discover how alive and dynamic consciousness is.

One thing that can help you stay with whatever you're experiencing is to realize that none of it is yours. The sadness and anger and pain are not yours; they're more like your inheritance from the world. The question is, Are you willing to meet this inheritance of pain so that you don't pass it on? If you never meet it, it goes looking for another place to be set free, either by those around you who you've dumped it on or even by a future reincarnational self (this is an idea I hold lightly as a possibility). Is it really better to escape back into judgment than to feel the sadness or whatever? Is it really so bad? It's not so bad because it's real. Just get curious about it. What's it like before you label it pain or sadness or anger?

The invitation is to get curious about the range of consciousness you experience each day. As you get curious about that, you might also notice that sometimes consciousness contracts and sometimes it expands. Ultimately, the suffering doesn't come from where your consciousness is but from the effort to hold it in one place or make it open when it's closed. Just be curious about wherever you are.

It's not up to you where your consciousness flows or whether it expands or contracts. Neither is right or wrong. Get curious about both of these possibilities. Expansion and contraction is just the nature of consciousness, like breathing in and breathing out.

It turns out that this flow towards what is, is what you are. You can't shut it off. So, if it really doesn't matter whether your consciousness is expanded or contracted, then you don't need to make an effort to either expand or contract it. If there's no effort, then there's no suffering. Discover what isn't harmed by being contracted. This flow is having a blast either way. Liberation is giving everything you've got to whatever you're experiencing.

The Life You Are Given

Our suffering doesn't come from any experience but from our resistance to the experience. Likewise, our joy doesn't come from any experience; it comes from our deeper nature. It is an innate quality of our Being.

There's a book out there with a great title: *The Life We Are Given* by George Leonard and Michael Murphy. So much of the time we don't show up for the life we're given but for the life we think we should have been given. This effort to have a different life is actually the cause of our suffering. It turns out that our joy doesn't stem from circumstances either. It comes from just being with the life we're given.

In hearing this, we naturally conclude that the way to end our suffering is to stop resisting. However, trying to do anything about your resistance is just another attempt to change the way things are. The only thing to do about this dilemma is to simply be willing to experience it.

A good metaphor for being with your experience in this way is trying to grow something. If you're trying to grow a plant, you don't go out in the yard every day and tug on it to get it to grow faster. Instead, you're just present to the plant, to its natural unfolding. You provide the environment for that growth to take place. You water the plant and fertilize it, but you don't actually do anything to the plant. Doing something to the plant itself could actually harm it.

The flow of conditioning is not a mistake. Part of this conditioning is the feeling that something is wrong with an experience and it needs fixing. As a result, it's counterintuitive to approach the cause of our suffering with other than the attitude of trying to fix it. We have to learn to let it have its natural rhythm and evolution and yet be very much in contact with it.

So, I'm inviting you to do some inquiry—to inquire into everything that's in the life you are given and not to change it in anyway. Because the suffering in our lives is caused by our attempts to change things, the inquiry I'm suggesting is an inquiry into whether or not that is happening, without doing anything about it. Inquiry into what is here right now is like picking the fruit that's ripe: Instead of going to the apple tree in the spring and being disappointed because there are no apples, you go to the strawberry patch and enjoy the strawberries—because strawberries are what *is* here.

All of our suffering is just our conditioning, and that's part of the life we are given. No one grows up without conditioning. The surprise is that there's just as much joy in being with conditioning as in being with a transcendent experience or profound realization. Because this joy is more obvious in a spiritual experience, we often make the mistake of thinking that it comes from a spiritual experience, when actually it comes from just meeting that experience, which is easy to do in the case of a spiritual experience. There can be just as much joy in meeting our conditioning, but we have to be willing to do this even if our conditioning doesn't change. We have to be willing to let it change in its own season. Some fruit ripens in the spring and some in the fall.

Regardless of what is arising, liberation is here right now. The invitation is to inquire into what is arising—just because it's here and not for any other reason. If conditioning is arising in you right now, even if there's conditioning to try to fix or change things, that's the life you are given right now. There is no better life. There is no better service than to fully experience your life and find out the truth of it. Inquire into it without trying to get rid of any part of it; it may not be the season for that part of life to ripen and be done. And yet, even when it's not the season for apples, you still water the apple tree. So, even if it is not the time for your conditioning to end, you can still give it this gift of simply seeing it, truly looking at what's here. That will help it ripen.

Where Is Your Attention?

We usually think that suffering is caused by bad experiences, but it's actually caused by our attention flowing towards something that's not really there—towards something that's not very true in that moment, such as an idea or a fantasy, which are very small truths. Suffering ends when our attention is flowing towards what's actually happening, what's true in the moment. Suffering is the distance—the gap—between what you're oriented towards and what is. However large the gap is between what's actually happening and what you're putting your attention on is how much you will suffer. If there's no gap, then there's no suffering.

That gap can be present regardless of whether something good or bad is happening. For example, if someone close to you is dying, your awareness may be so fully focused on what's happening in that moment that the experience lacks the suffering you would expect, although suffering may appear later if thoughts creep in about how things should have or could have been. In contrast, there are times when things are going really well and you're suffering, often because you're afraid of things changing. If this truth is understood—that it doesn't matter what happens—it can change your life. It may or may not change what's happening, but it will change your experience of what's happening.

Some of the things we might be oriented towards in the moment are very small truth such as hopes, dreams, desires, fears, doubts, and worries. When we give our attention to something that isn't actually happening, such as these things, we suffer. When our attention is focused on these things, we never feel satisfied because they don't nourish us. But when we give our passion and curiosity to more of what's true in the moment, we don't suffer. What are you giving your awareness, your passion, your curiosity to?

It's very simple: Our suffering is a matter of how much of our attention is flowing towards what's not actually present, such as hopes, dreams, desires, fears, doubts, worries, ideals, and fantasies. What we're desiring isn't present or we wouldn't be desiring it. Nor is what we fear. Our fears are just as much of a figment of our imaginations as our dreams. None of these things are real, and turning our attention towards the unreal brings us out of contact with the real, where the aliveness of Being can be experienced.

Rejection and Desire

Rejection and desire are the mechanisms with which we resist what is, which results in our suffering. The nature of rejection and desire is that either they're both operating at the same time (because if we're thinking about how great things would be if they were different, we're essentially rejecting things the way they are) or they're operating in a cycle: We go back and forth from rejection to desire. We think: This isn't good. Maybe if I got this or maybe if I meditated more or if only I had a better lover or more money or more freedom, it could be better. Then we go about trying to fulfill that desire and, regardless of whether we succeed or not, we come back to the point where we still reject whatever is present now. Even when we get what we think we want, we may find that it's not that great, so we dream up something else we believe will make things better.

This activity of desiring what isn't present and rejecting what is, is what creates and sustains the sense of a small self. If things are lousy, they're lousy for whom? For *me*. And if things could be better, better for whom? Better for *me*. We're often not even conscious of rejecting and desiring because we're caught up in the content of our desires and fantasies. We get so hypnotized by our fantasies that we're not even aware they're contracting our sense of self and making us feel very small, incomplete, deficient, and unsatisfied.

Nevertheless, that sense of incompleteness can be trusted. It's telling you how true it is that your fantasy will make you feel better. The sense of incompleteness and smallness in the experience of fantasizing shows you just how little truth there is in your fantasy. Fantasies aren't very true. They only exist in our minds. There isn't much substance or reality to them.

Self-Consciousness

One of our favorite ways of taking attention off of what's true in the moment is by putting it on the *me,* which is a very convincing figment of our imagination. We're constantly checking, How is it going for me? You've undoubtedly had many experiences of being so involved in something that, for a moment, you forgot to check to see how it's going for the *me,* how the *me* is doing, or how the *me* looks. You forgot to be self-conscious. We've all had moments of pure consciousness, when we were totally involved in whatever was happening. Athletes talk about "being in the flow" or "being in the zone." They don't really know how they do what they do because there's no self-consciousness, only consciousness—just what is.

You've also undoubtedly had many experiences of being painfully self-conscious—even when things were going well. A wedding is a great example: It's supposed to be one of the best moments of your life, but because it's so full of self-consciousness, it often falls short. We constantly evaluate our experience, and when we do this, we split ourselves off from it.

The problem with putting attention on the *me* is that the *me* is just a thought; it doesn't actually exist. If you just stop for a moment and look, you won't be able to find this thing called *me.* Whenever you look, there's something different there. It turns out that the *me* has no substance; it's just an ever-changing set of ideas. It's made up of thoughts about *me.* So, when you check to see how

I am doing, essentially, you're checking to see how a thought is doing. No thought has ever had a thought. This flow of consciousness is rampantly having thoughts, but the *me* within that flow has never had a thought. The *me* is just one of the thoughts appearing in that flow. And yet, all day long, we're checking: How's it going for *me?*

All that is real is experience; there's no container for experience called *me*. So, as long as your attention is flowing towards this *me*, no matter how many good experiences you have, you'll suffer because this is a place of contraction, a place that doesn't include the full breadth of your Being.

When you hear this, it's natural to try to be less self-conscious. But the only way you could do that is by becoming more self-conscious. As long as you're referring to how it's going for *me*, you never get to rest. The antidote is not something you can do. It's what you *are*, and it's right here, right now. You are pure consciousness, and this is the one thing you can never become conscious of. It's the one thing that consciousness itself can't flow to. That's why we put all these substitutes in its place, like the idea *me*. When you actually go looking for consciousness, it's like trying to look into your own eyes without a mirror. You know there are eyes there, but you can't see them. They're not hidden, but you can't see them. We know there's consciousness, but we can't see it or taste or touch it or hear it.

There's nothing else but pure consciousness that is having the illusion of suffering. When you see that, then that is the end of your suffering because that's the end of the *me*. All the *me* has ever been is your suffering. It's not such a great deal, is it? You get to exist but at the cost of suffering. All the *me* is, is this effort. Without the effort, all that's left is the wonderful play of pure consciousness called life, no one to experience it and no one to suffer from it; and yet it dances beautifully.

Noticing and Allowing

There are two simple instructions, or invitations, in satsang. The first is to notice your experience: Really notice what's happening right now. The second is to know that it's the right experience. Whatever you notice, whatever you find, that's the right experience. You thought you had to fix it or improve it, but it turns out that whatever you are experiencing right now is the right experience. A friend of mine has a friend who answers every question about how things are going with "Right on schedule!"

You don't have to wait to do these steps. You can start right now. Notice your experience—what's happening? Bring your awareness, your attention, your curiosity to bear on your experience right now. Secondly, just allow that experience to be the way it is. Stop the endless effort to try to change it, to make it better or different or more or less. Just let it be the way it is.

To the extent that you're doing those two things, there will an absence of suffering. And, of course, the opposite is true: You will suffer to whatever extent your attention and curiosity are focused on what is not or to whatever extent you are trying to fix, change, resist, or avoid this moment.

Actually you can't do either of these completely unless you're doing the other, so these two instructions are really only one. You can't fully notice your experience if you're already trying to change it or get rid of it. And you can't fully allow and embrace your experience if you're not paying attention to it.

One thing that's not required is seeking the right experience. The instructions are not to notice a particular experience or to notice an experience you've heard about or read about or once had that you want to have again. It's simply to notice the experience that you're having right now. There's no need to seek or search for a better experience than the one you're having.

If, however, in this moment, you are desperately trying to get a better experience or resisting the one you're having or paying attention to some idea about how things should be instead of how they are, then that's your experience. You don't even have to go to battle with that. Just notice what that's like.

What is it like when you're lost in a juicy fantasy about how great life will be if only this or that would happen? Or a juicy fear about how terrible life will be if this or that happens? The invitation is to notice what that's like rather than resisting that fantasy. Just notice what it's like to fantasize. Include the *experience* of being lost in longing and searching and fantasizing as well as the content of your fantasy. What is the *experience* of being lost in an idea? The point isn't to stop having ideas, which isn't even possible, but to simply notice what that's like. When you stop and notice, you find a lot of fantasizing going on. Most of us have an ongoing mental commentary going on about how our lives could be better or worse. What's that like when your attention is involved with these ideas?

We're always noticing something. I challenge you to not pay attention to anything for the next ten seconds. You can't do it. Noticing just happens. It turns out that these two simple steps are qualities of your Being, not something extra you have to do. Noticing is always happening, even if all we're noticing is the content of an idea. The invitation is to let that noticing take in more—take in the actual *experience* moment to moment. It may seem like a doing at first, but in the doing of it, it's more like you're being done, like you're being noticed along with everything else.

The same is true with allowing your experience: It is also natural to your Being. Right in this moment, your predominant experience is allowing. In this moment, the vast majority of what's happening in this room is okay with you. You're allowing the walls of this room to be the way they are. You're allowing the furniture to be the way it is. You're allowing your breath to breathe the way it is. In fact, you can reject only one aspect of your experience at a time; the rest is naturally allowed. You can only resist one thing at a time.

These two simple instructions are not something you need to do. The point in speaking about them is to get you to notice that noticing and allowing are already happening. This space of allowing is already present. It's so present that it even allows us to be in battle with what is. That's something you can get curious about. How much am I allowing what is and how much am I struggling against what is? What is it like if you just allow yourself even to not allow?

The Myth of Better

We are conditioned to believe something that has very little truth to it, so little truth that it's more accurate to call it a myth: We believe that things could be better. We deeply believe that we can have a better experience or a better life or become a better person. And, of course, the flip side of this is that we believe that things could be worse.

One clue that this belief is a myth is that not everyone agrees on what's better or worse. There's always someone who thinks the exact opposite of what you think. You don't even have to look to others for such contradictions: What you think is better or worse is always changing. What you once felt was good often becomes bad and vice versa: One day you think it would be better to be in a relationship, and then when you're in one, you think it would be better to be alone. The fact that your ideas about better and worse are so variable is another clue that this is a myth. *Better* or *worse* are just ideas with no substance or final definition.

The effort to try to make things better or to avoid something worse is our suffering. In order to hold the idea that something would be better, you have to narrow your awareness. Take the example of a relationship: In the beginning, we're all masters at narrowing our awareness onto all the good qualities of the other person. This narrowing of awareness is effortful, and it causes us to suffer. This struggle is not natural, so awareness doesn't stay contracted. Just naturally, our awareness expands, and we see not only the advantages to being in a relationship but the disadvantages.

Or vice versa, for example, if we've been avoiding something we consider bad and then it happens, with time, our awareness naturally expands to realize that it's not all bad. Those who've experienced something like cancer often speak about the advantages, the tremendous blessings in their life, from having cancer, even when they may be dying from it.

No one can keep the illusion of better going constantly because of the effort it takes to keep awareness narrowed; so it naturally eventually expands. When this happens, it often feels like waking up because the experience is so different. You wake up out of your particular dream of better, and it's often a huge relief. You wake up, for instance, to the fact that you're in a relationship with a real person, and it's both good and bad. Then, if you still choose to move forward with that person, you're doing it with more truth, with your eyes wide open.

We're so used to operating from this conditioning that even when we wake up from one dream of better, we usually latch onto another, although the next illusion may be subtler. For instance, you may now see that a million dollars won't make your life better, but you still believe that enlightenment will, so now you suffer over that idea. Or you might think that life will be better if your internal state were different—if you felt this way or if you didn't feel that way.

What would it be like to be here without referring to any ideas about what would be better or worse? What would it be like to be here without moving towards something "good" or away from something "bad"? It's possible that just as much would happen in life. Life wouldn't stop. What would it be like without any extra effort and struggle?

When we stop creating the division between good and bad, we begin to experience all of what is instead of just half of it. Our perspective is more complete because we're no longer denying half of it. Having ideas about better is like having blinders on. What you see with blinders on is only a part of the truth. If you're aware of the blinders, then there's no problem if, for a moment, you step into just a part of the truth. At times, it's even functional, like when you're balancing your checkbook: It's better to add up the numbers correctly. If you're willing to explore and question the underlying assumption of better, then you can hold this idea more lightly, with more flexibility. Then, if the numbers don't add up right, it's not a big deal.

The other question to ask is, Who is it better or worse for? Not only does the idea of better or worse make our experience very narrow, it makes the sense of our self very small. In order to even hold the idea of better or worse, there has to be a *me* that it will be better or worse for. Whenever you take on the idea of better, you feel very small.

You also have to watch out for the idea that it would be better to never think in terms of *better* or *worse*. The myth of better is so much at the heart of our struggle and suffering that even when it's pointed out to us, our tendency is to turn that into a struggle as well. This myth is functioning all the time. It won't go away and it doesn't have to. Just become aware of it and learn to be flexible about it. Sometimes it's necessary to step into the idea of better for a moment, like when you're at a restaurant and you're handed a menu. But if the idea of better starts to be believed or becomes fixed, the sense of your self becomes very small and you suffer.

What is it like when you do have an idea of something being better? By the way, none of these ideas are yours or your fault. They're just what you've been told all your life, which is why there are so many opposite ideas within each of us. What's it like when you take on a small self? That small self is just as mysterious as a larger experience of your Being. The experience of this small self, this contracted state, is not any better or worse than the experience of more of your Being; it's just different.

How many different small selves we all have! Every one of your ideas of better is related to an idea of who you are: If you think it's better to get drunk and bust up a bar, there's an identity that goes with that. And if you think it's better to sit in meditation and be in touch with Peace and Being, then there's an identity that goes with that—an idea about who you are.

What's it like when you just give up your ideas about how things might be better and your concern about how things are going? Things are always different, but they're never better or worse. That anything could ever be better or worse than the way it is, is an illusion.

It's all a question of what you are devoted to in this moment. Are you devoted to things being better or to what's real, what's true, what's really going on? There's no judgment here because there's a richness to the experience of having an idea of better and striving towards that. However, the possibility exists for that striving to release and to realize that striving isn't very relevant—you've been devoted to better your whole life, and you still haven't gotten there. You've been devoted to avoiding worse, and it still comes around. Even when you do reach something better, it's never enough.

When this is seen, it's possible to get in touch with a deeper drive, or longing—the longing to know what is really true. Rather than getting rid of any of the ideas about better, just let your devotion get bigger. It's still fine to try to make your life better in practical ways. The important thing is where your devotion lies. What are you really devoted to in your life right now? Is it the biggest truth?

Besides, do you really know what is better? You've taken it all on faith. You've believed what others said was better, but right now do you really know what is better? You don't really know what would make your life better or worse. So, now what? You don't know. What's it like to not know? Life doesn't grind to a halt. In fact, there's something very alive about this place of not knowing. When you don't know, you look around a little more. You're more present to what's really going on.

Without the idea of better, you can know things just for the joy of knowing things. You can know, for instance, the difference between one shade of green and another. They're different, but one isn't better or worse. When you're not narrowing your perception onto an idea of what's better, you're free to experience the richness of life and take in the differences. You can start to really enjoy whatever you're experiencing without the added layers of your ideas about good or bad. When there's no idea of better, there's no relationship to the world; there's just the world.

Am I Willing?

A great way to get in touch with your resistance to what is, is asking the following questions: Am I willing to have the experience I am having right now? and Am I willing to not have the experience I am having right now? If the answer is even slightly no to either of those questions, then suffering is present. This is a very high standard because it means that you have to say yes to every experience you're having right now and yes to every experience you're not having right now. One of our favorite ways of saying no to our current experience is fantasizing about all the other experiences we're not actually having. We often think we should be having some other experience than what we're having.

Fantasizing about the past is another way we keep ourselves outside of our present experience. The truth is that every experience you've had you've managed to lose. You're already losing the experience you're having right now, and a new one is taking its place. Are you also willing to lose every experience you have?

These questions help to broaden our focus so that we're not just noticing what's happening but also our relationship to what's happening. They broaden your focus to also include what's moving in you in response to whatever is happening—is it willingness or unwillingness? Is it a yes to this moment or a no?

When you ask these questions, what you quickly discover is that basically the answer is almost always no. Either grossly or subtly, there is usually a no there. For example, you might be willing to have a lot of money, but you aren't willing to lose it. Or you might be willing to have an experience end, such as an illness, but you're not willing to have it.

If you pay attention, you'll discover that trying to manage your experience is what your life is about. We are always trying to have the right experience by saying yes to the right ones and no to the wrong ones. When you practice this inquiry, you begin to see how much of the activity of your mind is caught up in resistance, in saying no to something. Even wanting something is a form of saying no to the way things are. When you are wanting something to be different, are you willing to have it be the way it is? No.

Nevertheless, there are moments when we experience an aspect of our Being that says a big yes to it all, to whatever is happening. In those moments, willingness is present, but it doesn't feel like *you* had anything to do with that. The suffering goes away, but we didn't do it. In hearing this, we may get excited: "I get it—I just have to stop resisting." But this is just another way of saying no—this time to resistance—and this will cause you to suffer as much as ever.

What I'm pointing to with the inquiry question "Am I Willing?" is not so much this dilemma (which you can't do anything about, because anything you try to do would just be more resistance) but another way of being with your resistance. Can you ask this question simply to see what's there? We're not very familiar with being with our experience in this way. Most of the time, our questions are in service to trying to get something to be better. What about asking this question just to find out what's there? Just touch your experience without any added push or pull, without a sense of trying to change your experience. This isn't a denial of your experience or an attempt to transcend it so that you don't have to experience your suffering. You're bringing your experience into focus but not doing anything about it. You're just experiencing it with an openhearted curiosity about it as it is.

What's it like to have the experience of resistance? In the space that this inquiry opens up, it's possible to discover a surprising thing: This big yes even shows up for our resistance. There is a place in our Being that is perfectly willing to have any experience and perfectly willing to resist and therefore suffer. In touching our resistance this gently, just letting it be the way it is, it's possible to touch more of our experience. To whatever extent we can touch our resistance, it's possible to see what else is present. Space is given to our *whole* experience, beyond the struggle and dissatisfaction created by our various strategies and ideas about what we should and shouldn't resist, what we should and shouldn't allow.

This question, Am I willing? illuminates the endless flow of unwillingness that is our conditioning. This is what we were all taught to do. We've all been programmed to say no to this and yes to that.

It can be helpful to realize that none of your conditioning is your fault. All of it is inherited. Our parents, our teachers, our spiritual teachers, our friends, TV, and the books we've read have all contributed to the ways we resist. They've all been telling us what to say no to. The beauty is, if you've been around long enough, you've been taught to say no to everything, to opposite things: Don't be poor and don't be rich, don't be proud and don't be self-effacing, and on and on. If you get to know your own conditioning, you discover how contradictory it is. That's why you never got it right—because when everything is wrong, nothing is right.

In the midst of this conditioning is the big yes that you can't make happen. There's no technique or process for bringing you to a place of that wholehearted yes. And yet, just by being willing to experience your suffering and struggle in this moment, you can discover that this big yes is also present. Nothing has been gotten rid of: Your conditioning is still present, but the view has broadened to include this Presence that has no problem with any experience nor with the resistance to it. Paradoxically, you discover that being willing to see all the ways you say no, opens the door to experiencing what is always saying yes.

This open-handed, openhearted gentle way of touching our experience and our suffering is counter to how we've been taught to respond to things. We've been taught to see everything as an opportunity to decide if something is good or bad for *me*. For example, you notice the weather, and immediately you decide if that's good or bad. Everything from the most personal to the most impersonal event in our lives is put to the question: Is that good or is that bad for me?

Spiritual inquiry is about another possibility, which is to just touch your experience without any push or pull. If what happens when you do that is resistance, then you just touch *that* experience. You never run out of opportunities to just be curious about your experience as it is.

Liberation from suffering isn't dependent on our resistance being gone but on the recognition of this big yes, this willingness to allow whatever is. Liberation isn't the absence of resistance but a meeting of that resistance and a recognition of the underlying big yes present in every experience, including resistance. For that, you don't have to do anything, you don't have to add anything, you don't have to get rid of anything.

Of course, the part of you that has been conditioned to try to make your life different is going to take these words and try to make them into something you have to work on, something you have to learn to do right. But guess what? Being has no problem with you taking these words and using them to suffer. Can you open yourself to the devastating truth that Being has no problem with any of your suffering?

Are you willing to find out what is here and to touch it, to touch your own experience? Are you willing to touch your conditioned resistance? With the discovery of this big yes, our conditioning shrinks back down to its actual size, which allows us to see it more clearly. This seeing shortens its lifespan, while resistance doesn't. Touching your conditioning without any expectation speeds up its dissolving, while resistance keeps it intact. Our conditioning needs this gentle, curious touch in order to be seen in perspective.

This bigger yes is not something we do or practice or accomplish. It doesn't come out of our doing. It's an aspect of our Being. It's really a description of Being itself, whose nature is *yes*. Its nature is love. Its nature is acceptance. This *yes* is not something it does; it just is that *yes*.

The nature of this bigger yes is all-inclusive, it has no opposite, and it's fundamental. It's a fundamental aspect of what you are. It's already here. You don't have to do anything to have it be here.

In contrast, let's look at the experience of *no*. What's the experience of rejection like—not wanting something, not liking something, thinking something is bad? This *no* is something you have to assert: You have to speak up or act to get rid of what you're rejecting.

Worrying is one example of how we say *no* to experience. It's like *no-ing* preemptively or preventively. All this rejection is simply a mental activity. As a result, it doesn't have a lot of effect. Our worry doesn't prevent anything from happening. We try to get rid of a lot more things than we have ever succeeded at getting rid of. We have all kinds of strategies for how to prevent something, and then it can happen anyway.

The same is true of our *yes-ing*. We spend a lot of time idly wishing and hoping, saying yes to things that aren't even here. But this is just more mental activity. Sometimes those desires are strong enough that they spill over into activity, and we work real hard to get what we want—a new lover, more money, a spiritual experience. Most of the activity is still in our thoughts, though, and the world doesn't always comply with what we want.

Life doesn't refer to your ideas about life. Life has a much bigger playbook than the one in your mind. A lot happens that you do want and a lot happens that you don't want, and yet there is all this mental yes-ing and no-ing and trying to figure out what you should be wanting and what you shouldn't be wanting. Why so much effort for so little results?

Contrast all this effort to the innate yes, which is the nature of that which is aware. Just like water is wet and fluid, the nature of this space around experience is that it's aware and loving, and it says yes to everything; it's embracing of everything. It even permeates all of this activity of mind. Right there in the midst of all of our drama and struggle and effort, there's something saying "yes—okay let's worry now." This *yes* gives life to whatever is there. If a worrying thought is there, it enlivens even that. That's why our mental constructs are so entertaining—because even they are imbued with this aliveness of Being.

This *yes* is present in everything; it's more prevalent than air and more intimate than your own skin. It gets into every nook and cranny, and it is every nook and cranny. It's already there. It's already here. It's inherent in every expression, whether it's a mental expression, a physical activity, or an act of nature. Every desperate longing and fear is actually imbued with awareness, this overarching embrace, this *yes,* which is your nature. This is quite a contrast to the usual way we say yes to things. It's much more fundamental.

Be Here Now

"Be here now" is a classic spiritual instruction, which essentially means to be in the present moment. It points towards something that is already true, towards something that is unavoidable. It's like me telling you to sit the way you're sitting. You're already doing it. You're already being here now. No one has ever successfully left the now. If I told you to be somewhere else now or to be here some other time, you can't do it. It's too late to be somewhere else than *here.* When you just stop and look, you see how ridiculous it is that you could be anywhere else than here or that you have to do anything to be present in the now. Then, why do we even talk about it?

We talk about it because there are two kinds of nows: There's the real now, the now that is happening, and what you could call a fake now, a made-up now, one that doesn't really exist. Instead of experiencing the real now, we're often experiencing our fantasies about the now. We experience something that's not really happening. It's like we go to sleep and have a little dream in the now, an experience of a non-existent now. Anytime thought is occurring, you're experiencing something that's not really happening. Even if I talk about something wonderful, like Liberation, what happens is you go inside and have a fantasy about Liberation, which is not what's happening right now. It's a made-up now.

We narrow our attention onto an idea about something that's not here in an attempt to make it be here. We think that if we fantasize enough about something, it will happen; as if, for instance, fantasizing about a spouse or roommate picking up after him or herself will actually make that happen. We live in an internal, magical world, like the world of a young child, where we believe our wishes have the power to change reality.

Our capacity to fantasize is like having a machine that prints counterfeit money. We've all been desperately printing off counterfeit realities, and they don't do us any good. Our fantasies never work, we can never buy anything with this fake money—it's got Mickey Mouse on it instead of George Washington. It doesn't do us any good.

Even when the instructions "Be here now" are given, the mind can turn it into something to do. It then creates a fantasy of what being here now would be like, and we experience that fantasy. That's what happens when we *try* to be here now.

At other times, we either forget to generate a fantasy or we're just so exhausted from the effort to maintain our fantasies, dreams, illusions, preferences, and ideas that for a moment we collapse from that effort and land in the real now.

Rather than turning this instruction into something you have to do—you have to stop fantasizing—the invitation is to experience whatever you're experiencing now, even if what you're experiencing is a fantasy. The point is not to shift what you're experiencing now but to actually experience it. If what you're experiencing now is the veil of illusion being ripped aside, exposing the real now in all of its glory—great. And if what you're experiencing now is a thick veil of fantasy, conceptualization, and desire—separation from the real now—great. Then, *that's* your experience. The invitation is to really experience that because that's the experience you're having, so it's the only one you can have. The alternative is just not available right now.

When we're desperately trying to experience the reality of these unreal things, there's never any satisfaction, only dissatisfaction. Trying to make your fantasies real is never satisfying. Paradoxically, when we fully experience the inherent dissatisfaction of our hopes and fantasies, that is satisfying. It's so satisfying to be real, even if that means being real about the fact that you're lost in an unreal thought. Satisfaction lies in what *is* happening. By being willing to show up for whatever experience you're having, you begin to experience the real now. Only when you show up for the emptiness of your dreams do you get to experience the fullness of what *is* happening in that moment—the sound of the birds, the light in the room . . .

When you begin to include more in your awareness than the content of your thoughts and fantasies, you realize the fullness of now. Now is ridiculously full; it contains everything, including your fantasies. It's not only there in your fantasy; it's also here in reality. The now has no limits, both in terms of space and time. It includes everything that is. *Now* already is everything that was and everything that ever will be. So, what do you want to give your attention to—an empty fantasy or this bursting reality?

This isn't meant to suggest that you should try to change the fact that you have dreams and fantasies and hopes. This ability to imagine other possibilities is a great gift. Practically speaking, it's very useful to be able to generate an image of something that's not present. For example, if someone says to you, "Meet me at my house at noon," this ability to imagine gets you to the right place on time. However, the value of this ability is limited.

In addition, this capacity to experience a fake now also serves us by allowing us to experience the fullness of the real now through contrast with the emptiness of a fake now. If there weren't this capacity to live in illusion, then it would be meaningless to talk about living in reality. There is no way to distinguish the experience of reality unless you also can experience unreality. This is the reason we create illusion: It eventually makes us connoisseurs of reality.

Hopelessness

One thing that happens when you orient towards the present moment, towards what is really happening instead of what isn't, is that hope is destroyed. Life also destroys our hope as it reveals the truth. Have you ever noticed how life doesn't seem to refer to your hopes and dreams? When you live long enough, every hope, dream, desire, and ideal you've ever had gets dashed. They get dashed even when they come true and you find out your dream wasn't the answer either: You get a million dollars, and you're still miserable. You get a wonderful relationship, and you're still restless. The truth about your hopes, wishes, and dreams is that they don't get you anywhere.

Seeing this would be simple if we never got anything we hoped for because we'd quickly lose interest in hoping and desiring. The problem is that occasionally we get what we hope for, and that is powerfully reinforcing, powerfully addicting. We become addicted to our hopes and dreams. We desperately struggle for a few intermittent rewards. The complete reality of hoping is that it's mostly a horrible experience.

There are lots of lies behind our hopes. For one, we assume that if we get what we hope for it will be forever. That's the whole fairytale ending: "and they lived happily ever after." We never look at the whole truth, which is that everything is always changing, and everything that comes is going to go.

Another lie is that we believe that life will be a certain way once our dream is realized. But, of course, everything in life has both a good and bad side: We get a million dollars and it only messes up our lives. Life is never as simple as our hopes lead us to believe.

A third lie is that we think that hoping, dreaming, and wishing will make us more active and productive, but does it? It actually takes up a tremendous amount of time and energy. We think that hoping is what makes our life go somewhere. Without it, we think we will be passive and do nothing. We don't see that life happens regardless of our hopes and dreams.

The biggest lie is that we believe we'll be happy when our hopes are realized. But our hopes are like ordering a dessert from one of those dessert trays: It looks really good, but when you bite into it, it's often stale and flavorless. When you actually bite into all those hopes, dreams, and desires that have driven you for so long, you find out they don't satisfy or if they do, it's the kind of satisfaction that's never enough. A friend of mine used to say: "You can never get enough of what doesn't really satisfy." Hoping and desiring are like a hunger that can't fully be satisfied.

We tend to follow our hopes and desires away from what's real. We keep trying to satisfy them, but each time we try, we move farther away from what's real, and what is real is the only thing that can satisfy us. This is a description of every addiction. Every time you get a fix, it satisfies less, so the next time, you need a higher dose. When you go in that direction, the connection to what's real gets thinner and thinner, and the suffering gets worse and worse. It gets to the point where you're not experiencing any satisfaction, just a temporary relief from the pain and suffering of hoping.

It's not a mistake that we get so addicted to our hopes. Strangely enough, that's the path to our salvation. Ramana Maharshi used to say that no one ever wakes up from a good dream—you wake up from your bad dreams. Sometimes there's no other way to find out the truth of your hopes and dreams than to bet all your money on them and discover that, win or lose, they still don't satisfy.

Another possibility is to be willing to look at your hopes and see what is really true about them: Are they satisfying? Are they bringing something real and fulfilling into your life or are they taking you farther away from what's real? What are you choosing right now? Are you choosing something that will lead you to the truth or something that will fuel that underlying dissatisfaction? In this moment, one of those things is happening: you're orienting towards what is real and true or you're orienting towards a hope or a dream.

When you show up for the experience of hoping, you realize that what you're hoping for is not real, it's not here, it's not happening. This dissolves the hope because once something is exposed as having little truth, it becomes uninteresting, irrelevant. If I say, for instance, that there's a hungry tiger in this room, you aren't affected because it's obviously not true. When you actually show up for one of your hopes and discover that it's as unreal as this tiger, the juice goes out of it. Nothing is driving it anymore. Your hopes turn out to be empty. Once the truth is seen about your hopes, you can't delude yourself anymore.

Even though, it's a big relief to lose all your hopes, that is, to see that there's no point to them, there's often tremendous resistance to letting go of each and every one. The reason this is so is that we don't really see how it's possible to be without them. Instead, we sometimes replace them with despair, which is really just a negative hope. Rather than hoping for something wonderful, despair is like hoping for something terrible. We fantasize something terrible happening in the future. So, for most of us, the experience of being without hope is the experience of despair.

Why do we do that? One reason is we think that that will motivate either ourselves or others: If we're afraid, we expect that to motivate us to do something about it or to get someone to take care of it for us. This pattern became established because occasionally it worked, especially when we were little. When we were afraid, we discovered that sometimes we got taken care of. Another reason we do this is that it gives us a sense of knowing what's going to happen, which often seems better than not knowing, even if what we think is going to happen is negative. We also do this because it adds drama to our lives. Without hope and despair, what is there to struggle for or against? Like hope, despair is just another strategy for managing the future.

The good news is that being present to whatever is happening not only deconstructs your hopes but also your fears. And life, of course, does that too. Often from shear exhaustion from so much hoping and despairing, you come to a place where you are hopeless and despair-less. You've lost all your hopes, and you're not replacing them with despair. You're not filling in this moment with hope for a better moment or fear of a worse moment. You're just experiencing the absence of hopes and the absence of despair.

That experience is an experience of emptiness. When you begin to pay attention to the content of your mind, you notice how much of it is a hope or a fear. Imagine if you saw that all of your hopes and fears have no relevance, no reality, no truth. Because that's been the focus of so much of your attention, when your hopes and fears become uninteresting and irrelevant, life can seem empty initially. Now what? What's left? What's left is reality, which is always rich and satisfying. All striving and dissatisfaction disappear in the now, and what appears is completely satisfying.

When you finally stay in the emptiness, then it's possible to see what's beyond your hopes and desires, and you notice that there's a lot more going on than your grasping. There's much more to the now than what's arising in the mind. Life is and always has been unfolding in incredible ways, and our desires and hopes have had very little to do with that.

Telling the Whole Truth

There is power in speaking the truth. Speaking the truth is often what therapy is about. Some have suggested that speaking the truth *is* the therapeutic process, that the actual speaking of what is happening is therapeutic in and of itself. There is an assumption in therapeutic processes, however, that what needs to be admitted to or confessed is what's wrong, what's not working, what's not comfortable, what's not easy in your life. In satsang, we suggest you talk not only about what's wrong or even what's right in your life but also about the most subtle and profound truths of your experience. Satsang is a place where you can confess the full extent of your Beingness.

There are also times when the only way you can truly express the breadth and depth of your Being is without words. Silence is the only thing big enough. So, silence gets included as part of the confession that can happen in satsang.

There is great power in admitting the whole truth, even if words are not needed. What would it mean to admit to things that are complete? What about the sunshine? Is the sunshine complete? We can admit to the sunshine. We can confess the glory of the light coming into this room, every shade of color and shape and form that our eyes are taking in right now are a blessing of that sunshine.

If you just take it as it is, is your body or anything else a problem in this moment? There may be lots of sensations and things happening right now in your body, but right now what a miracle it is just to have arms and legs and hair and toenails. What an amazing thing to have toenails! And ears. And teeth. What an amazing thing! How much of the experience of your body right now is like the sunshine?

And what about the more subtle parts of your experience? What would it mean to confess the content of your Heart right now? How rich to have the capacity to be touched so deeply by the joys and sorrows of life! What an amazing thing just to be here and have this capacity to be affected by words, by sounds, by the sunlight, by the experience of having a body—to have something that registers all of that. What a miracle! Are you willing to confess that?

In this moment, can you also admit what an amazing development it is to have problems? It seems fairly unique to humans. What an amazing thing to have an experience and then have an idea of how it should be, to actually create that tension or that split. What richness! There's no particular drama to the sunlight in this room, for instance, but you could have a drama about it, such as wishing you were outside in it instead of in this room.

One of the things we humans are touched by is this conditioned capacity to struggle—to have an idea of how things should be in the midst of this amazing wonder of Being as it is. You can be in the middle of a room with this much sunlight and what's really going on is you're struggling with the question of do I have enough love or do I have enough money or whatever, even though in this moment we are all fabulously wealthy with sunlight. We have sunlight to burn. We have so much we could waste it! In the midst of all that richness, we can also have the rich experience of lacking something. The invitation is to include this in the confession of what's happening.

What power there is in speaking about all of it! It puts everything in perspective. When you speak your problems, all of sudden they are actual size. For example, no matter how annoying something someone does is, the truth is that it's only annoying while they're doing it. That problem is really only so big. Seeing a problem in perspective makes room for discovering other ways of being with it.

It's a demanding practice to speak the truth. It demands being willing to admit our humanness and how in the human dimension we are limited and evolve gradually. It also demands being willing to admit that our humanness is not the whole truth. Speaking this out loud often allows that admission to take on depth and breadth. How much of the range of what's here right now are you willing to admit? To admit any of it is an amazingly courageous thing.

Love Is Always Here

To admit the whole truth means recognizing that love is always present. Much of our suffering comes from one simple misunderstanding: that love is limited, that it is here only some of the time. This is a misunderstanding about the true nature of love. Love is actually the container for everything else. It's always present. Love is that aware, allowing space in which everything happens, so it's present no matter what happens. It is so completely loving that it allows everything, even painful emotions and negative thoughts.

Realizing this truth ends all striving and struggle and, consequently, all suffering. We no longer need to strive to create circumstances where love will be present. It's already here. You just notice the space of allowing that has always been here.

Once you realize that love is already here and never goes away, it no longer makes sense to strive to make things be other than they are, no matter what happens, no matter what comes and what goes. Something can come into that space or leave that space and the space is still there. The love hasn't been added to or diminished by either the coming or the going.

What is it that you're really looking for in getting love from another person? You're looking for space. The perfect lover is someone who allows you to be whatever way you are. If you're in a good mood, the perfect lover would allow that. If you're in a bad mood, the perfect lover would allow that too. And yet, that perfect lover—that perfect love—is already here. It is already allowing everything.

What really nourishes us is simply recognizing this love—the endless giving of space to everything that happens. That allowing, or accepting, is the nature of our Being; and when we simply notice that, we can experience this limitless love.

Everything Is Perfect

The truth is that everything is perfect just the way it is. Right here, right now. That's pretty simple. You don't have to go searching for perfection. You don't have to do anything for it. It's already here. Nothing is missing in this moment. But there's more to it than this: This perfection is always changing; it never stays the same. It's never even the same way twice. It reinvents itself every moment as a new perfection. It's very alive.

Given this, you can see why it can be so challenging to keep recognizing that everything is perfect. You finally see the perfection of a particular moment, and when you look again, everything has changed and it may not seem so perfect anymore. Somebody rear-ends your car—this is perfection? You get a letter from the IRS—this is perfection? You become depressed—this is perfection? Even when something better than we imagined happens, it can be challenging because it messes with our idea of perfection. Perfection turns out to be much wilder and crazier than your idea of perfection. It goes off in all kinds of directions that you wouldn't necessarily include in perfection if it were up to you.

For many, the recognition of perfection comes when their awareness is expanded and they step outside themselves for a moment. Then, perfection is obvious. As a result, spiritual techniques have been designed to do this in order to help us realize core truths, such as the perfection of everything.

You can imagine how misconceptions develop from this: The sense of perfection becomes associated with expanded states, and we begin to think it lies only there. So, we get busy seeking these states in order to get our dose of perfection. But, like everything else, these states come and go. Rarely does someone stay in an expanded state when, for instance, they get a flat tire.

Fortunately, the recognition of perfection is not dependent on your state. There's nothing wrong with expanded states, but the effort necessary to try to maintain them is exhausting and can interfere with experiencing perfection in very simple moments, even in a contracted moment. When you're busy trying to hang on to a state, you're not seeing that perfection is in every state and every experience. If there's perfection in the Whole, then why wouldn't it be true of every part of the Whole? What if it's possible to realize the perfection in everything that happens and in every state that comes along? What would that mean? How would you approach your experiences?

Think about the way you approach your spiritual practice now. You probably approach it with a degree of sacredness—you create an altar with pictures and flowers, light a candle, sit in a particular posture, and close your eyes. All of that is done in honor of the perfection—the truth—that is revealed through that practice. What if everything is revealing truth to you? What if everything is revealing the perfection? Wouldn't it make sense to approach everything with the same sense of sacredness, with the sense that every moment is worthy of your full, undivided attention?

If all your experiences are facets of this perfection, why would you leave any of them out? Every experience that comes along, even losing track of perfection, can be experienced as perfect. You can approach the experience of expansion and the experience of contraction with the same sacredness. Every experience is not only imbued with perfection but made of it.

You're never done recognizing this perfection because the perfection shows up in a new and completely different way every moment. The recognition of perfection is more about cultivating a sense of wonder than experiencing an expanded state. Without the willingness to meet everything with wonder and curiosity, you miss many parts of the perfection of this wild, strange, and mysterious thing called life. The perfection is much, much bigger than anything that can be contained in our ideas about life. Even if we've experienced a lot of this thing called life, life always manages to surprise us. Are you willing to be surprised again and again?

ABOUT THE AUTHOR

After a lifetime of spiritual seeking, Nirmala met his teacher, Neelam, a devotee of H.W.L. Poonja (Papaji). She convinced Nirmala that seeking wasn't necessary; and after experiencing a profound spiritual awakening in India in 1998, he began offering satsang with Neelam's blessing. This tradition of spiritual wisdom has been most profoundly disseminated by Ramana Maharshi, a revered Indian saint, who was Papaji's teacher. Nirmala's perspective was also greatly expanded by his friend and teacher, Adyashanti.

Nirmala is also the author of *Living from the Heart, Meeting the Mystery, That Is That, Gifts with No Giver,* and other writings that are available as free downloads on his website: www.endless-satsang.com. In addition to giving satsang throughout the U.S. and Canada, Nirmala is available for Nondual Spiritual Mentoring sessions in person or over the phone (see below). Nirmala lives in Sedona, Arizona with his wife, Gina Lake. More information about her and her books, including *Radical Happiness: A Guide to Awakening,* is available at www.radicalhappiness.com.

About Nondual Spiritual Mentoring

Nondual Spiritual Mentoring is available to support you in giving attention to the more subtle and yet more satisfying inner dimensions of your being. Whether for a single spiritual mentoring session or for ongoing one-to-one spiritual guidance, it is an opportunity for you to more completely orient your life towards the true source of peace, joy, and happiness. Nirmala has worked with thousands of individuals and groups around the world to bring people into a direct experience of the spiritual truth of oneness beyond the illusion of separation. Mentoring sessions are offered over the phone and typically last an hour. To arrange an appointment, please use the contact form on http://endless-satsang.com.

Printed in Great Britain
by Amazon.co.uk, Ltd.,
Marston Gate.